HAPPY
OCTOBER 15TH

The true story of love, loss, and the strength to continue.

Copyright @ 2016 Carmen R. O'Brien
First Edition, August 2016
ISBN: 978-1536906998

Dedication

This book is dedicated to my amazing husband, Bill.
Hand in hand we walked this journey. I love you.

To my amazing girls: Shayla and Melaina.
You are my world. I love you more than words could ever
say.

To my parents: Delbert and Elaine
You were there with us during the darkest times.
Your support and love mean more than I could ever repay.

Happy October 15th.
As I sit in the ambulance making yet another trip to the hospital, I can't help but wonder how it turned out this way. You read the books. You lose yourself in a good story. Sure, every good story has a conflict. All issues are solved and everything comes out just peachy in the end. The woman gets the man and they live happily ever after. The lawman/lawwoman catches the bad guy/gal and saves the day – just in the nick of time. Heck, The Brady Bunch had a crisis that was solved in less than 20 minutes; and, they had a crisis every week!

For some people, life can sail along quite smoothly. They don't have much more than a "Bradyesque" type of problem. Who really broke the vase? Will Jan be voted 'Most Popular Girl'? To those people, I am envious. Unfortunately, that hasn't been my reality. Life's questions can't be answered in that short amount of time with words of wisdom by Mike Brady.

So as I sit in the ambulance, I have to ask myself how I got here. How many more times will I be here? And, on a more selfish note, when will it be my turn for the good news; for the smooth sailing. I want the scenario of meeting Desi Arnez Junior because my housekeeper knew his housekeeper.

Chapter 1

As I sit in the back of this ambulance, I can't help but be grateful. That may sound weird to most people. No, I do not have Munchausen by proxy syndrome. No, I do not get delight in the pain of others. I just never thought I'd be here. I am worried. I am frustrated. I am a wreck. I am thankful. I am in this ambulance with my daughter. A child we were told we could never have. That's why I'm grateful. I wish like hell this wasn't her 3rd ambulance trip. I know she will be okay. I don't want her to go through this. We (my husband and I) have been through this before and we will get through this again. She will be fine.

When you are growing up, are you ever really prepared for what life can throw at you? I don't think so. Those cruel realities just didn't exist. With my hometown being so small, there were no real problems growing up. Everyone had larger families. We all knew each other. Crime was a thing for people who lived in New York. That's real life, though, isn't it? There are no real problems. It's a Hallmark card.

Maybe my parents kept us sheltered from them. Maybe people just didn't talk about things like they do now. I'm not sure. What I observed was this - you grew up, went to college, met the man of your dreams, had a family and lived happily ever after.

I don't know about you, but growing up was rather idyllic for me. I was the youngest of 4 children and the only girl. I was raised in Whittemore, Iowa. It's a very small town - at the time it had only 700 people. There are even fewer people living there today. It was a Mayberry of sorts. We lived on 7th street which was the last street in town. Across the street and behind the houses was a cornfield. Like I said, it was small town Iowa. We played kickball in the streets and learned how to do cartwheels in the vacant lot next door. We safely rode our bikes all over town. Every summer day was spent at the city swimming pool. It was safe and tranquil. Everybody knew you and your parents.

I attended a Lutheran parochial school through my 8th grade year. I also attended Camp Okoboji. I went for a week every summer starting when I was 9 years old. I loved camp. I made some very good friends there. Some people I am still friends with today. It was that sort of place. (Some people I have lost track of and wish I could find.)

For high school, I made the 10 mile bus ride to Algona. I went from eight people in my class to 185. I guess it was like starting over. I did well in high school. I was on the honor roll 14 out of 16 quarters. (Darn that physical science and the teacher!) I was a basketball cheerleader. I had two best friends, Becky and Julie. We did everything together. (I am happy to say we are still friends to this day!) High school was, high school. Were they the best years of my life? Absolutely not! I had some fun. I wanted what most other girls in high school wanted. It seemed like almost everyone got what they wanted, except me. Girls in high school just want a boyfriend. Someone she can go out with on Saturday night; someone who would hold her hand and give that class ring to some day. Those were my friends' high school days. I had no real boyfriends. Let's face it; I had a crush on the guys way out of my league.

I always knew that staying in Whittemore or Algona was not what I was going to do. I wanted that college degree. I wanted to move on to different places and things. I wanted more. I also knew that staying there was not going to get me my happily ever after. It was time to move on. I was off to college. First on the agenda was a degree. Maybe the other would be found on my journey of higher education.

I was going to college to a place where no one else from my high school was going. That was the way I wanted it. I could be me and reinvent myself or just start all over. I did have some friends going there from camp, so I wouldn't be alone. My brother was attending there as well. I had family and a few friends at my new school. At the end of the summer, I packed everything I needed into my brother's car. My mom cried as we pulled out of the driveway. I felt a little sad at that moment, but I was on my way to being a college student 3 ½ hours from home.

I attended Concordia College, St. Paul. (It's now Concordia University.) I loved my college and the time I spent there. I was a cheerleader. I played softball and intermural basketball and volleyball. In the summers, I would go back to Whittemore. I was a Lifeguard at the same pool where I had spent so many summer days. While at Concordia, I met some of my closest friends. We did so much together. We cheered together, studied together, and, yes, even partied a bit. I cherish those memories. I was very active. I did OK, but not at the Dean's list level. That was a shock. Everything in high school was so easy. I didn't even have to try. I was not prepared for the intensity of college. Being away from home, all the distractions; there was just so much to do! I had some brief relationships in college but nothing that was lasting or substantial. As a young college female, I did wonder if I would ever meet anyone. People are meeting that someone special all the time. I was thinking that was just a grand illusion. How do people even find "the one"? How old would I be? Would it really ever happen for me?

I had originally gone to school to get my secondary education degree. I wanted to teach high school grammar. After four years of college, I was ready to be done. If I wanted that secondary degree, I would have to go another year. I had the elementary credits, so I chose to go that route instead. I thought I could always go back and get the secondary degree, if I still wanted it, at a later time. I graduated on May 31, 1983, with a degree in elementary education and an emphasis in English. I was a licensed K-9 teacher. I had the credits to be a parochial school teacher, but I could also teach in a public school. If I went the church teacher route, Concordia would do the placement and help me get that first job. I went back to Whittemore for the summer. I was hoping it would only be a month or two and I would get my call and off I would go to change the world, one student at a time!

That call came at the end of July. I was asked if I would like to teach second grade in Rochelle, Illinois at the Lutheran school. (I was also the volleyball coach, cheer coach, and dance coach.) I had no idea where Rochelle, Illinois was located. It had to be by Chicago, right? Isn't everything in Illinois located with reference to Chicago? I could do this. I found it on a map and I went out for a visit. My brother, Steve, went with me for company and to help with the driving. We toured the school and I found an apartment. A couple of weeks later, I packed everything I owned into the back of my 1972 Ford Galaxy (a college graduation present from my parents) and started the 400 mile journey on my own! I was brave. I was tough. I was outgoing. This would be no problem.

I WAS SCARED TO DEATH!

I remember driving on the overpass as you enter Rochelle. I started to cry. I was tired. I was scared. It was ugly. I said to myself I would only stay a year and get out of there and move closer to home. I went to my little one bedroom apartment above a house and unloaded my stuff. All I had were clothes, personal items, a TV, a stereo, dishes and a sleeping bag. The first night, I slept in the sleeping bag on the floor and cried. I was scared and the closest person I knew was 7 hours away.

My parents came the next day. We shopped for curtains, pots and pans and other household items I would need. We stayed at a hotel that night. It was not a good beginning. I was running a fever and was pretty sick. Was I really sick or was I just that scared? I think it was more of the latter. When we went to my apartment the next day, my apartment was completely furnished! The church had taken donations to furnish it! Maybe this wouldn't be so bad after all. For some reason, I started feeling just a little bit better. I am a strong, independent woman. I can handle anything. But remember, I was still only going to stay a year. Maybe I should think about staying two. It would look better if I didn't move around too much.

That year started out very lonely. I would teach school, go home and watch tv. My tv was a small black and white portable one. At least I had cable. My weekends consisted of cleaning an apartment (which didn't need it) and church on Sunday morning. For months and months, that was all I did. I sure was living the life. Not really. I was lonely and I was stuck.

I made several trips during that first year to St. Paul to visit college friends. I even made the 7 hour drive once a month to see my family. It was a long trip to make alone. I had to see friendly faces and people I cared about. At times the loneliness was overwhelming. I would leave on a Friday after school, around 4 p.m. I'd stop at the convenience store on the way out of town and get a large drink and a bag of chips. Once I hit that highway, I didn't stop for 6 hours. I did that every other month for quite a while

In the spring, one of the other teachers found out I loved softball. He "forced" me to call the park district and get on a team. He said if I didn't make the call, he would. I called the park district. They asked if I wanted to be on a very serious playing team, partying team, or one in the middle. I wanted to be on a team that was decent and maybe win a few games, but still liked to have fun.

They had the fun part down. Our team was terrible. We may have won one game that season. The record didn't really matter. I was out of my apartment and meeting people. I met a lot of people. I played shortstop and Joy played first base. We may have been the only ones on the team with softball experience. Maybe it was because of that, or maybe because we were the only single ones on the team, but we became instant friends. Joy and I started hanging out together. We went out on the weekends with another friend, Jan. The next year we were recruited to a different team. We won the league. Maybe Rochelle wasn't so bad after all!

I met and had a serious relationship with one person. He broke my heart. Who am I kidding, he shattered my heart. We met through the softball league. (His brother was one of our coaches.) We had dated for several months when he had asked me to move in with him. I refused. I was a teacher in a Lutheran school after all. There was no way. Despite that, things were really going well for us. Then, one day, out of nowhere, he found out that an ex-girlfriend had a baby. She didn't tell him about it. He found out from somewhere else after the fact. He wasn't even sure if it was his. But, it doomed our relationship. It was over. He couldn't deal with it. Men...well, men. They can't handle much. He said he loved me, and then said he lied. What the...? Rochelle didn't seem big enough for the two of us. I was thinking it was about time to move away. Get my name on that call list again and move on to the next adventure. I wasn't getting any younger!

I had just started my 3rd year of teaching at St. Paul's when I met Bill.

Chapter 2

Joy had spent so many weekends sleeping on my couch that we decided maybe I should move and we could share an apartment. Being a Lutheran school teacher, my salary wasn't very large. Sharing an apartment would be cheaper for me. We pretty much did everything together anyway.

We would spend every Sunday watching the Chicago Bears at a restaurant/bar just outside the city limits. Bill had known Joy through a girl he used to date. He would come into this bar on Sundays when he was out 4-wheeling or something similar with his friends. He would talk to Joy, but not me. After a while, we started talking a little. I would see him more frequently on the weekends. I thought he was a lot of fun. When we saw each other, we would joke around. It wasn't a big deal, but it was refreshing. It was distracting from the relationship that scarred me. Maybe a little fun was in order to forget the past and move on to something new.

One night at our old hangout, I was walking around the bar on my way to the ladies' room. He literally picked me up and put me over his shoulder. He took me outside and set me down. That was it. That was interesting. That was weird. The next Friday, he asked me if I would like to go on a date this Saturday. I said "Yes". I thought it would be fun. At this point, I was just trying to move on. I didn't even know if the pieces of my heart had come back together. Everyone told me that if I was looking for something serious, Bill was not the one I should go out with. He was fun, but don't expect much more than that. He was not the type to settle down. That was perfectly fine with me! That may be just what I needed. I was still pretty gun-shy after that last relationship. At this time, I was afraid of serious. A little fun and no pressure could be just what the doctor ordered. After the fun of this was over, maybe I could move on or literally move out. While I had met some great friends, I was still thinking that maybe it was time to move on. Get my name on the call list and completely move. A little fun in the meantime wouldn't be such a bad idea.

Our journey started on November 1, 1985. That was the day of our first date - a triple date to be exact. Kenny and Nancy, Danny and Penny, Bill and I were the crew. All six of us loaded up into Bill's 'white whale' (that's what he had named his car) and headed off to DeKalb, Illinois. It was a great time. We went to a movie. We saw "Better Off Dead". Not the best movie I had ever seen, but it did have its humorous moments. After the movie we all went to Sergeant Peppers for pizza and to have a couple of beers.

Bill and I saw each other every day after that. He would stop by at night just to tell me goodnight and give me a kiss before going home. Then he would stop by in the morning for another kiss and to tell me to have a good day. He sent me flowers every Friday. Some days I would go out to my car after school and find a card on the steering wheel. Once a found a stuffed bear sitting there. He actually wrote me a poem and put it in a card. What a romantic! My head was spinning and the butterflies in my stomach were going crazy!

A mere 2 ½ months later (just 11 weeks, on January 18, 1986) we were sitting in the old hang out. He looked at me and said, "Why don't we get married?" I said, "OK." And there you have it. Not the most romantic proposal, but we were engaged. We set the date. It was set for July 18, 1987. That would give us a year and a half engagement. That sounded about right. The engagement came fast, but it gave us time to plan the wedding. I won't say it was without a little drama. Shock from some people, whispers from others, but we knew it was right.

This was the guy that everyone said would never get serious! We went together to pick out a ring. I went back and forth between it being a surprise and letting him pick it out or to have me pick out my own ring. He told me that I would be wearing it for the rest of my life, so I had better find the one I liked. After that day, Joy told me it was too late to back out now. I had a moment of panic. Was it too soon? Was he really the one?

Yes, he was.

I won't bore you with wedding details. My parents said that if we were married in Whittemore, they would pay for the wedding. It wouldn't be easy making long distance plans. As it turned out, it wasn't bad at all. My mom was great with details and I didn't freak out about the small stuff. We were going to get married at my home church in Whittemore, but we had a major disagreement with the pastor. I left a meeting with him in tears. I told my parents I would not be married by that man. I had a friend who was a pastor in Burt, Iowa. It was 20 miles from Whittemore. We had it approved by their elders and we were allowed to be married in Burt.

It was a HOT July day, but the day turned out great. His friends were crazy. We may be the only ones in the history of that church to have a mannequin attend the wedding. It was quite the party and nothing major went wrong. We were a happily married couple.

After the wedding we had a week-long honeymoon. We drove up the western side of Minnesota and into Canada. We drove home on the eastern side, through the Boundary Waters and along Lake Superior. It was beautiful. With that behind us, it was time to settle into our storybook lives.

Let the fairy tale begin.

We moved into a farm house outside of Rochelle. The place was a dump. In exchange for rent, we fixed the house up. We cleaned, painted, wallpapered and put in a new kitchen floor. We made it livable. We even went to the shelter and got a dog. It was a scary transition. I'm not going to lie. It was all a little strange to be living with this man in a different place. It would all work out.

I was no longer teaching. We had gone through some rough times at the school. Our principal was inadequate. Our 5th-6th grade teacher was inept. People started pulling their kids out. My class was going to be very small so they combined 1st and 2nd grades into one classroom. The first grade teacher was also the music director for the church and school. I was just a coach. She was offered the job. I was without. Before, when I wanted to leave, I didn't. Now, when I wanted to stay, I couldn't. This was something we could get through. This wasn't the end, but a new beginning.

Our lives were just beginning and we had so much to look forward to living together for the first time; being responsible adults and planning a family. It should be easy. We would just wait a little bit and then try for our family. We didn't want to wait too long. After all, Bill was 25 when we got married and I was 26. According to some, I was practically over the hill and past my childbearing years! We decided we would wait 1 year before we would get pregnant.

Nice idea anyway.

One October day, just three months after the wedding, Bill came home and said, "Let's move." He was working out of Aurora, Illinois. He was leaving for work around 4 a.m. and getting home about 9 p.m. His boss would not let him take a shorter route. This was not good for us newlyweds. We had very little time to spend together. I was working at Walmart, Casey's, and substitute teaching. The house, even with the work we had done, still needed so much more. The furnace didn't work. The owners wouldn't fix it. They wanted us to take care of it. That wasn't going to happen. It was old and needed to be completely replaced. I told him we would have to move anyway. There was no way we could afford all the fixing the house needed. The landlord wouldn't do it. We would have no choice but to find a new place. He said, "No, let's move to Iowa." I couldn't believe he just said that! Of course I would like to move closer to my family! His family was still here…all 11 of the brothers and sisters! I told him it was up to him to tell his parents and let everyone in his family know that this was his decision, not mine. I did not make him move away. Outwardly I was calm and rational. Inside I was ecstatic.

Two weeks later, we were living in Cedar Rapids, Iowa. We had both gotten jobs. I thought getting another teaching job in a bigger city would be easy. Boy, was I mistaken! I started working in the mall. Right after Christmas I switched to an office job. Bill was working for a tire company. We weren't rolling in the dough, but we were happy. We had made new friends. My high school friend, Julie, lived in town. Our new next door neighbors were Tim and Connie. They were fun! (That later turned into Tim and Vanessa.)

Life was good. There was only one thing missing.

Chapter 3

One day, after we hit our 9 month anniversary, we were sitting at home and Bill said he thought it was maybe time to try for a family. I was a little shocked and frightened. This was a big step. I had just turned 27. Our relationship seemed solid. We weren't getting any younger. It may take a couple of months, maybe even a whole year! Why not? When those pills ran out, there was no refilling. We were on the road to becoming parents! It was scary but so exciting at the same time! We had a plan! I was sure by the next Christmas we would either have a baby or baby news to share with the family. Well, that was how we saw it working. No one told us that sometimes things just don't work out like you had planned.

We heard a lot of folktales, old wives tales, and all sorts of other tales that really meant nothing when it came down to getting pregnant. A year went by without achieving our goal. That was acceptable, I guess, but it should have happened by now, right? Was there something wrong? There couldn't be. My mom had 4 kids without any issues and Bill's mom had 12! I was not some skinny little rail who had issues every month. I was born to have babies. These hips were made for it!

Just relax. Everything would come in due time.

In May of 1989, we purchased our first home. It was a small ranch house in Hiawatha. It was a dirty mess. We could see the potential. We bought it and worked on making it better. The work was fairly cosmetic, with the exception of a new furnace, central air and duct work. It took a lot of elbow grease and paint. It used to be an upper and lower duplex that had been converted to a single family home. We would concentrate on the main floor and, hopefully, fix up the basement down the road. It had 3 bedrooms, one 'finished' bathroom, and a full basement. It had plenty of room to grow. We could take our time and get that done. It was a perfect starter home for a family. Bill joined the Hiawatha volunteer fire department. With all this going on, it really helped to keep my mind off the 'other issue'. However, that never seemed to leave the back of my mind. Since we had taken this step, surely it was a sign that we were ready.

Bring on Baby!

I said, "Bring on Baby!" That was not going according to the plan. That should be the easy part. Did I need to draw a picture? Getting pregnant should be easy. People have been having babies since the beginning of time. Everyone just assumes that when you are ready to take that step – and sometimes when people really aren't – you can get pregnant. Sometimes it took just a little longer. Sometimes it took longer than it should. The advice we got was so helpful. You just need to relax. Take a trip. It would happen.

Well, it didn't! And, nothing happened for another year. And, nothing happened for another year! At first, we didn't think too much of it. Sometimes it could take a year or more. I had been on the pill for a while. We would take our time. We owned a house. We had jobs. We were really settled. Things were going well. This was the next phase of our lives. It would just happen. Then it didn't. We started thinking it should have happened by now.

After we'd been married a few years, people started to question when we were going to have kids. So, that made us think about it some more. We tried harder. It was just getting scary and frustrating. It was always in the back of our minds – maybe mine a little more than Bill's. A family was what I thought about. We went to work. We paid our bills. We had a social life. However, this idea of starting a family and why it wasn't 'just happening' never really went away. I didn't understand how this wasn't going according to our plans!

The longer it took, the more people seemed to think you needed their wonderful words of wisdom and snide comments. They actually thought they were being funny and had the right to say whatever crossed their minds. "Aren't you ever going to have a baby?" "What's taking you so long?" "What's the matter; don't you know how to do it?" "Does Bill need me to show him how?" "I don't understand. All I had to do is put my husband's shoes under the bed and I was pregnant." These comments, and so many more like it, were not welcomed. After having to listen to these comments myself, I vowed I would not ask others the same or question their family plans. Certainly, I had no advice to give them when it came to getting pregnant anyway. All those lovely sentiments really hurt my heart. It was the fuel to my self-loathing, bitter disappointment and failure.

When I was asked when we were going to have kids, I used to respond with "Not tomorrow, I'm busy." They would usually laugh and that would be the end. I wasn't laughing. People didn't get it. They didn't understand how their words could sometimes hurt. They didn't understand that it was not a joke. They didn't understand the monthly disappointment. The constant reminder that, once again, you had failed. As a bonus, you get to have a period, complete with horrible backache and severe cramps!

Congratulations!

After a few years, I was moved from my regular OB-GYN to a fertility expert. Oh goodie. I was not excited to see an expert. The fact that I even needed an expert to get pregnant was ludicrous! People got pregnant every day. What was wrong with me? Why would I need a specialist? My dreams of having a family seemed to be dwindling each month. What would happen to our marriage? If there was a problem with Bill, would I want out? If it was me, would he want out? Children are a big part of marriage. It's up to each couple on how many they want. They can choose to have none. They can choose to have 15. As long as you can take care of the ones you bring into the world, go for it. Bill loves kids. I've always wanted kids. If I couldn't do this one simple thing, would he find someone else who could?

The appointment was set. As scared as I was of being branded a loser in the world of fertility, I was also sure this would really get things going. I was going to be pregnant by next Christmas for sure! You pray. You pray harder. You cry. You pray. You pray harder. You try.

Nice try.

Chapter 4

Next came all the testing. It all started with the temperature chart. I had to take my temperature every morning before my feet ever hit the floor. This needed to be charted. The doctor needed to see that rise or spike in my temperature. That would signify ovulation. If there was no sign of ovulation, a little pill would take care of that! If my temperature went up, there was ovulation. When the temperature went back down in a week or so, I was not pregnant. Month after month, chart after chart, appointment after appointment, and nothing happened. The temperature went up and always came back down. Part of that was good as I was ovulating. Part of that was horrible as I still wasn't pregnant.

It was time for further testing. There was the hamster test. The hamster eggs are closest to a human's. The sperm is tested with the hamster egg to make sure that it can penetrate the egg. We did that. We got a call. The control was bad and we need to do that one again. Are you kidding me right now? Once was bad enough. Back to the hospital we went. It turned out to be OK.

Whew!

I had an endometrial biopsy. Yeah, that hurt. They wanted to make sure the endometrial lining could support a fertilized egg. That turned out to be acceptable. To be perfectly honest, we were both tested for more things than I can even remember. I was a pin cushion. If you have modesty or are extremely private, I'm afraid fertility testing is not for you. At least back in our day it wasn't. Maybe they have taken huge leaps today, but everything was slow, exhausting and expensive.

If you are not a fan of schedules, then infertility is definitely not for you. I know, like you have a choice in the matter. Be ready. If you want to continue, to go through the testing, to go through the charts, mark down every little thing you do as far as reproducing, there was a schedule for virtually everything. I had to do the chart. It was every day, without fail, the first thing. I marked down my temperature on a graph. I marked down each time we had intercourse. Oh, and we couldn't do that whenever the mood struck us. We had to wait three days before ovulation. We HAD to do it on the correct day or we might miss our chance. Our romantic mood and emotions had nothing to do with it. We were to become these robots and turn it off and on. It was wearing on us both. We CAN'T tonight; it's too close to the time. We HAVE to tonight or we miss our chance. Once we hit this stage of 'the game' we were so not in control any more.

I am a control freak. This was hard, really hard. I will admit; it caused some tension between us.　Love and romance, well that was something on the back burner. This was reproduction. That was it; plain and simple. There was no place or time for feelings and romance. You performed according to the schedule. That may sound cold, but it was the cruel reality of the situation.

I will never forget one test I had done. It was the hysterosalpingogram – HSG for short. I was going through all these crazy tests and wanted to keep many private. I scheduled this one for my lunch hour. I went to the clinic. I went into the room with a thin robe on and nothing else. The purpose of this test was to look at my tubes. Were they open? Was there a blockage somewhere? Could my fallopian tubes function? They said it would be quick. An hour should be long enough. As I was lying there, dye injected into my system, feet in the stirrups, and the doctor came in. Gasp! He was not alone. He had students with him. He told the 4 or 5 students (it may as well have been 500) to "Step around and have a look. The female cervix is quite interesting." I could have died of embarrassment. He didn't ask me if it was okay. He just invited them all down. Why not choose some people off the street? Let's all have a look! After that humiliation was over, I went back to work.

A couple of hours later, I started getting a stomachache. Nothing too bad, but I just didn't feel well. By 4 o'clock in the afternoon, I was getting a fever and the pain was worse. By eight o'clock that night we were on our way to the emergency room. It turned out that I had an acute allergic reaction to the contrast dye used in the test. That was one of the first nights I got to spend in the hospital going through this fertility process. What joy! This just kept getting better. I guess the silver lining was that my tubes were good.

What a relief!

The fertility doctor prescribed Clomid for me. It's a fertility drug that can make you produce more than one egg. There was a chance of twins. That would be okay with us. After all this, we were game for almost anything. If we had twins, we would only have to do this once. We would have our family and begin to just enjoy our family. We were a little scared. We really want one baby, not a litter. We were ready to do it. We were ready to take our chances. Let's just get pregnant!

I took a Clomid. The very next day, I had pains. They weren't too bad, just a little twinge on the side of my lower abdomen. I am tough. I am woman, hear me roar! I took more Clomid. I took Clomid for months. All the while I had appointments. They checked my temperature chart. Each month there was a spike. Each month the temperature went down. Each month when my temperature fell, I cried. Once again I was not pregnant. Those days when the reality was another failure were the worst. I would be edgy and irritable. I would cry.

The problem and the reason for the pains in my lower abdomen…I had cysts. They were very painful. Every woman gets a cyst every month. Did you know that?

When the egg is released, it leaves a little cyst. They are very small and will either dissolve on their own or pop. Most women don't even know this happens to them. But for me, the cysts didn't dissolve or go away. The cysts filled up instead. The pains didn't go away.

One night the pains were very intense. I could barely stand. Bill insisted that we make a trip to the emergency room. I was not a fan of the emergency room. What if it turned out to be nothing? It took quite a while for him to convince me to go. As we were leaving, the pain was like an explosion in my abdomen and I fell to my knees. He wanted to call the ambulance, but I wouldn't let him. I told him I would go to the hospital, but only if he took me. So joy, it was another trip to the emergency room. It was a ruptured ovarian cyst. I got to spend the night in the hospital.

A few weeks later I had to see the doctor for a follow-up to my latest hospital visit. My close 'friend' the fertility doctor suggested that it was time to do a laparoscopy on me – just to get a closer look at what could be going on inside. Ok, let's do that. It was scheduled for Halloween. I went in at an ungodly early hour. It was my first surgery. I was thinking it would be the only one I would ever need. (Joke's on me!) It was a pretty quick procedure. He told me he cut away some scar tissue and drained six ovarian cysts. Great! That should do it then. All the issues had been resolved. In a month or two, we would get ready for baby!

Not so fast.

Six weeks after my surgery, I had to go back to see the doctor. I still had terrible pains in my sides. I didn't feel well. It was so hard to even stand up straight. After talking to me and finding out what was going on, he leaned out the door and asked his nurse what he had going on the next day. He told her to cancel everything and for me to be at the hospital at 5:00 a.m. I was going to have surgery in the morning! That didn't leave me much time to notify work. I may be off for one day and up to three weeks. It just depended on what they found and have to do. I was told to plan for another laparoscopy with the possibility of doing more. What did that even mean?

I thought a quick surgery date wouldn't be so bad. I mean it didn't give me much time to freak out and worry about it.

I got to the hospital and surgery prep began. I saw immediately that they were not preparing for a laparoscopy; they were prepping for major surgery. This was when I became a little frightened. The anesthesiologist told me he was told to be prepared for more than a simple probe. I was told if I woke up in the recovery room, it was the simple procedure. If I woke up in an actual room, they had to do more. It was a good thing I got to sleep through this or I would have been a wreck!

I'm not even sure how much time had lapsed. I believe the surgery lasted about an hour and a half. I woke up in the elevator on the way to my room. I had in incision in my abdomen from one side to the other. There were over 20 staples in my stomach.

They did the major.

They drained and cut out three ovarian cysts. They are called chocolate cysts. They get their name because they fill up with old blood. They didn't pop. They didn't dissolve. They just keep growing. Your ovaries are about the size of a grape. One cyst was the size of a tennis ball. That was cut out. Then, they 'zipped' over to the other side to remove two the size of marbles. They also cut away more scar tissue.   This would surely solve the problem. Now all I had to do was recover from surgery. It would probably be a month or so, and then it would be baby time!

As I was lying in my hospital bed, they brought in a roommate. She was a 17 year old child that was 8 ½ months pregnant. Are you kidding me? She was there for some stress tests. She started going on and on how she should have had the abortion when she found out she was pregnant. She ranted about her boyfriend and that he accused her of still doing drugs. She said she hadn't done drugs for a couple of months now. She went on and on and on and on. I rolled over and cried. What was wrong with this hospital? Did they have no idea why I was there? Why in heaven's name would you put a 17 year old pregnant girl in a room with a 30 year old woman suffering from infertility? Hello? Just a little background check would have been beneficial. Bill came into the room. He looked at me crying silently in my bed with my back to the roommate. I told him what was going on. He immediately went to the desk and had words. She was moved. She was told having a roommate wasn't good for her stress levels. Bye bye. For the next 4 days, I was in the hospital. I knew it would be worth it. This time it was going to work!

Right? We thought so anyway.

Chapter 5

In the meantime, we thought we had better check out all of our options. There was a couple at our church who had adopted two children. One was from India and one was adopted from Des Moines! We made an appointment with them to talk about adoption. We were trying to be realistic. This may be our only option. If we wanted kids and God was telling us no, we may have to go this route. What we found out was even more discouraging. It would be a minimum of $10,000 and could take up to six or seven years to get a child. The people from church that we talked to were ripped off by another country's government. They were told they were getting brothers. The government kept the money and they never got their babies. They were out $20,000. That was crazy! That sounded worse than what we were going through! We thanked them for their time and kept the information. Our plan was to keep this on the burner – the way back burner. If we had no success by the time I was 35, we would go this route. Once we hit the magic 4-0, our chances became more remote of even being able to adopt.

We talked about the possibility of being foster parents. That conversation lasted about 10 minutes. I think it's very honorable and noble to open up your home to children who really need a home, stability and a caring family. Under 'normal' circumstances I would have maybe even considered it. I just couldn't stand the thought of having a child, caring for its needs and then giving it back; maybe to less than desirable conditions. I was in a selfish mode. If I had a foster child, I don't think I mentally could have handled giving the child back. My heart would have broken.

I will tell you, I am a church going person. This will rock your faith to the core. While all this was going on, my work invited a charity spokesperson to talk to us. They were looking for donations to fund their various projects. They told us the story about how they help young people who are having kids. They even had their first 11 year old that was pregnant! Are you kidding me? Are you serious? You should be teaching the kids to be abstinent! You should be encouraging these kids to see the beauty and selflessness of adoption. We should NOT be teaching KIDS how to become better parents! I understand that in today's times, it's no longer taboo to be a teenage parent. I understand that more teens choose to raise their children. If they are going to be responsible for this small life, they should know how to be responsible for it. I get it. However, that was not what my head nor heart was thinking. I was outraged! I did not give one penny to that organization and to this day have not contributed. It cut. It cut deeply.

Of course, when there was something you were struggling with, the whole world was after you. Every song, every TV commercial, every person you saw on the street was just another reminder of what a failure you were. I had never felt so helpless until then. Why would God even do that to us? We were good people. We had a strong marriage. We had been tested again and again. Yet, God allowed this 11 year old to have a baby. You hear of the horrible cases of child abuse. I would never do that! Why were those people able to reproduce? Here I was with no baby. I was angry! I quit going to church. I couldn't understand it. Why would this be our lot in life? It should be so simple. We wanted children. Get pregnant. I mean really, was that so hard? Was that so difficult? After all, 11 year olds were doing it. It was not my fault. It was not Bill's fault. We were doing everything under the sun. It must be God's fault. He was punishing us for some reason and I was pissed.

So there. Take that. You weren't helping. We would do this without You then!

I am normally a very happy person and outgoing. This situation has a way of changing you. It overtakes your life.

It's all you can think about. I wished that there was someone I could talk to. I wished there was something I could read. I wanted to know that I was not the only person out there going through this. I really felt alone. All my friends had kids and had no problems having kids. What was wrong with me? I just couldn't believe this was our reality. I even asked Bill if he wanted out; if he wanted to find someone who could give him children. He was appalled that I even asked him. He was in this marriage, this partnership, with me. WE would get through this together.

After months going by with no success, it was time to try something new! Yay. The doctor suggested to put me on stronger fertility drugs. There was an issue. With my history of cysts, I couldn't just be on this stronger drug, Pergonal, alone. It was so strong that I could blow an ovary. That was no joke. That sounded like some sexist joke, but the possibility of that was real. So, we had to combine that drug with another, Lupron. This drug would shut down my system completely and the other will stimulate the ovaries into mass production. The good news was there were 2 shots a day, every day. Yes, that was sarcasm. I just couldn't bring myself to sticking myself with a needle twice a day, every day. I asked Bill. He agreed to do it.

So here was the schedule for this one. I got two shots every day. I went to the doctor's office every other day while on these drugs. There they would take a blood sample and do an ultrasound to look at the egg production. When the eggs looked the right size, there would be another shot that would release the eggs. We then would have to go to the doctor's office for artificial insemination. That way there would be a better chance of fertilization. That was our plan and we were sticking to it. It sounded crazy, but it also sounded like it would work. I believed it would work. Ah, the romance!

First things first.

I literally had to go to the bank to get a personal loan. You had to pay for prescriptions upfront, along with needles for the shots and all that good stuff. I would get 80% of the prescription cost back through insurance, but it was that initial cost. Plus, insurance would not pay for the insemination. That was out of our pocket. I got the money and we were ready to go.

I went and stood in line to pick up the prescription. I will never forget the lady in front of me as she got her prescription. Her prescription was around $60. I gave them my name. They told me the total for the prescription was $580! That was just for the two prescriptions I needed right away. I wouldn't need the other until later. That one shot was about $100. I just looked at her and told her she thought hers was expensive!

Needles, prescriptions and a faith in modern medicine all in hand, we began. After that horrible time of the month was over, it was time for the shots. Bill gave me the two shots every day. Not extremely painful, but not pleasant.

Let me tell you, those drugs played havoc with my emotions – especially the Lupron. I sometimes felt so angry and frustrated that I just wanted to hit something. Sorry, but that's the best way to explain it. At times, I was so lethargic it was hard to move. There were days where tears would flow. It was like going through hell. But if it was hell that I must face to get this baby, then bring it on! I would go in to the doctor's office every other day on my lunch hour to have blood drawn and to have an ultrasound. That may sound bad enough, but I have horrible veins. I could get poked anywhere from 1 to 5 times per visit. It was not something I looked forward to or enjoyed, but it was necessary. At this point, I would do anything. Heck, I've already almost done everything! The blood work was for hormone levels and the ultrasound was to check for egg production and size. They would see how many eggs there were and to make sure they were of the correct size for release. The more eggs the better. It would increase the chances of at least one being fertilized.

Finally, the day came where we were told to get the drug, an hcg, for the shot to release the eggs. This was it! The insemination was strategically timed out and planned. I got the shot. We collected the sperm. I took it to the doctor. It was all very romantic. It was going to work.

I got to the office at the appointed time, specimen jar in hand. I got prepped. I was so excited! My uterus was jumping! I was going to get pregnant, finally! The insemination was completed. I was told to stay lying for a while...don't move! After an hour, I was sent home. I was to take it easy. The new baby would want me to. Then, we waited. I was to keep marking that temperature chart. We would see. That temperature won't go down. I will be pregnant!

So we waited.

Two weeks later, the temperature dropped. Two days later, the period started. Another failure. Don't be discouraged; said the nurse, we can go another round! Yippee. Let's do this all over again. It was just so much fun.

Off we went to the pharmacy to get that prescription filled. Back to being a pin cushion. The routine started all over again. I went back to the doctor's office every other day. I went back to hoping it would work this time. In the meantime, our friends, Tim and Vanessa, who had been married a shorter time, were also having a struggle with fertility. She, however, could get pregnant, but would have tubal pregnancies. I realized that was very dangerous and scary. I was thinking to myself - and this may sound very wrong to some people - but I would even take that. That would show me some hope. At least that way I would know I could GET pregnant! I would take a miscarriage...anything to show that it was a possibility. I absolutely mean no disrespect or cruelty to anyone who has suffered a miscarriage. It is a horrible ordeal. You want and love a baby that is no longer there. I have nothing but deep respect and sympathy for all who have lost a child this way. It is heart-wrenching. In my situation, I was looking for anything I could see as positive. I was getting nothing but false hopes and heartbreak. We had the parts. This getting pregnant thing should be easy. I just needed a sign of some sort - a little encouragement.

So, here we were into week 2 of the shots. I was thinking it was time for that miracle release drug. The ultrasound showed too many cysts. They wouldn't let the eggs grow. We would have to go another week. Another week went by. The ultrasound showed the same thing. We should give it one more week. Ugh! Ok, let's do that. The next week, it was the same thing. Back in the room, I was told this procedure would have to be aborted. The number of cysts, about 12, along with the size of them, made the egg release impossible. We would have to wait and start all over. I told her I was done! We were broke. My emotions and hormones were all over the place. I was a wreck. I cried all the time. The doctor came in and told us we would probably never be able to have kids on our own. We would need to do invetro or something similar. There was no way the two of us, on our own, would be able to get pregnant. That was what we were afraid to hear. I had this feeling in the back of my mind that children would not be in our future. Just hearing those words actually spoken aloud to me made my nightmare a reality.

He left the room. The tears silently slid down my cheeks. The nurse tried to be positive. She gave us the standard jargon. "Don't give up." "You have come so far." "Maybe just give it a couple of months and we can try it again." What about being broke did she not understand?

She told me there was another option. Oh goody, let's try something else. Everything had worked like a champ so far! She would give – GIVE – me three months of birth control pills. I was to take them without any down time. In some cases, if you don't give your body a chance for a period, it will 'hyper-ovulate'. That may increase our chances. I was thinking, "Sure lady, we have had so many positive results so far. Why wouldn't this one work?" I took the pills and went home. This was November 1992.

I took the pills for the first month. I didn't stop them to have a period. I wasn't upset by that little side effect! I was halfway through the second month of the pills, when our friends, Tim and Vanessa, told Bill they wanted to come over. I had this complete feeling of dread. I knew they are going to tell us she was pregnant again. I grabbed a beer or 3 or 4 and waited for their visit. I just wanted to be numb. I was right. They told us the news I feared. Not because I wasn't happy for them. I was just so miserable for myself, for us. (Unfortunately, she suffered her 3rd tubal with that one. I sincerely hoped she wouldn't have to endure that again.) I think I cried for hours after they left. As supportive as my husband was, I just don't think he got the empty, hollow feeling of failure. Let's not forget the periods every month that were like a punch to the stomach that you can't even do this right. Bill looked at me and said, "Let's just forget it. Let's stop everything completely. This is just too much for you, for us. You are a wreck. Let's take a break from it all and figure it out later." Was I ready to give up? Time was ticking. I wasn't getting any younger here. I would not admit defeat. I told him I had 2 weeks left of the free pills and then I would stop. Maybe take a year off from the miracles of drugs and science and give it a rest. I was 31 years old. Tic. Tic. Tic.

Defeated. Deflated. Barren?

Chapter 6

Two weeks went by. Yay, another period! Man, did I just love those. Mine were awful. Severe cramps, headache, back pains, heavy flow for 7 days. Good times. But, I knew this was coming. We were just taking a break. Those charts and thermometer could go in that night stand drawer and just stay there for a long time. I was sick of you. I was sick of it. As I stated earlier, for the most part, I am a pretty positive, upbeat person. I am very outgoing and laugh a lot. With all that we had gone through, I had gone through the spectrum of emotions. I was empty. There was no happy. There was no sad. There just was. I existed. We went through the motions of our daily life. Even though we made the conscious decision to stop, subconsciously it didn't. For 5 straight years it has been drugs, testing, shots, blood, ultrasounds, temperature charts, cash, cash and more cash and major disappointment.

It didn't just stop that easily.

I will say about this time I made some peace with God. Was I still upset that this was our situation? Of course I was. We had been through hell. We had faced it together. We were strong. With God on our side, anything was possible. I was raised as a church-going person. There was something missing when we didn't go. I don't want to get all preachy here, but we slowly made our way back. A few extra private prayers still wouldn't hurt. We had a few more years before all hope would be completely abandoned. Even though in the back of our minds, the possibility that we were done and childless still loomed.

In mid-December 1992, Bill and I were heading to a work party and were leaving the house around 10 p.m. He walked out in front of me and I was right behind him. I stepped off our porch, on to the driveway. I stepped on a small patch of ice. I heard a sound like multiple twigs snapping. I hit the concrete. Bill turned around to help me up. I told him not to touch me because I had heard my ankle break. I told him to go call his friends – the guys from the fire department. He dropped everything that was in his hands and went next door to call 911. It couldn't be broken, could it? I looked at my foot. The left foot was at a 90 degree angle.

I started to scream!

The neighbors came out of their house. They brought blankets and tried to block the December wind. Bill and the neighbor were going to pick me up to get me off the ice. All I could hear in my mind was high school first aid class teacher. "If a bone is obviously broken, don't move them. It could cause more damage." I wouldn't let them move me.

Next came the lights! When one of 'their own" was in need of an ambulance, the fire department came with every truck – complete with lights and sirens. We had 2 fire trucks and a rescue truck in front of the house. Add to that 2 police cars blocking off both ends of the street and an ambulance. It was chaos! A police officer was there and I can say I didn't like him – at all! I told him to get off my property. (Oops!) The assistant fire chief, Marc, was a very good friend of ours. I remember him straddling me and holding my leg. He did that so I wouldn't see it. They cut off my shoe and sock. It was very obviously broken. The bottom of my foot was pointing to the side. There were bones almost breaking the skin. He told them to get me the heck out of there and to the hospital. (I wouldn't know that until later.) I was put in a vacuum splint. Ahhh, that felt so much better. I was taken to the hospital.

At the hospital, they did a set of x-rays. A little while later, I was taken back for another set of x-rays. In the back of my mind I was thinking, "I'm going to feel really stupid if nothing is wrong with it!" There was such chaos on our street. I would be embarrassed if all that commotion was for nothing. The doctor came in. I asked him if I broke it. He said, "Oh boy did you! Do you want to see the x-rays?" He held them up and explained, "This bone goes here, this bone goes here and this bone goes here. This one is broken off and we won't know where it goes until we do surgery." Nice, it wasn't just one broken bone but 3 breaks.

But, that was not all.

My ankle was also dislocated about 1½ inches out of place. That would have to be put back into place immediately. Because we had eaten dinner about 4 hours prior, they didn't want to do surgery right away. They would rather wait until morning. However, if they couldn't correct the dislocation, they would have to perform the emergency surgery. The doctor grabbed my foot and tried to pop it back into place. I screamed! He asked the nurse to give me some Vercid. This drug is supposed to give you instant amnesia. They gave me a shot. To me it seemed instantaneous. I looked at Bill and asked when they were going to do it. He said it was done. I told him it wasn't that bad. He said I screamed and screamed. I didn't remember a thing.

Now that was a good thing!

I was taken to my room. Surgery was done at 7:00 the next morning. I had 6 screws and a plate put into my foot. I stayed in the hospital for 4 days. Following that, I was home for 5 weeks. The break was so severe; they couldn't get my foot to go in a 90 degree angle. My ankle was shattered. I couldn't go back to work until I got a walking cast or boot on my foot. It was 5 weeks of lying on the couch and sleeping there. Bill would get me a little cooler with juice and water before he left for work. I would have some crackers and fruit for lunch. I really didn't move much for 5 weeks.

That was not my idea of a good time.

After that time was over, I went back to the doctor. My foot was much better. I had no feeling on the inside of my ankle. He told me if it didn't come back in a year, it probably never would. He also told me that I would probably get arthritis earlier than normal because of the damage that was done. I guess arthritis at 50 instead of 60 wouldn't be that bad. I got in a walking boot and I went back to work. This was the second December in a row that I had missed work; last year for the abdominal surgery and this year for my ankle. They started kidding me at work that I was the best 11 month employee they had! I told them that the next December I would be there!

I should have known better than to make a promise too far in advance.

Chapter 7

In March, we made a trip to Rochelle to visit Bill's family. We had a good time with Bill's sisters and brother-in-law. There was alcohol consumed. There was no reason not to. On the drive back home, I looked at Bill and told him I was late. I was only about 4 days late. His response to this was that he didn't want to talk about it. We had been so disappointed too many times that why should this be any different. I let the subject drop.

Monday I went to work. It was work as usual. The only thing I noticed was that I was really tired. I mean REALLY tired. I may have 1 soda a day. My choice was Mountain Dew. I was drinking about 3 and the caffeine did nothing. It was Friday morning of the week after our trip to Rochelle. I was walking down the hall and I almost passed out. I thought to myself that there was something 'wrong'. I was still late. So I had a couple of choices. I could either be coming down with the flu. Or, could it actually be that I was pregnant?

I called Bill. I told him that I was going to call the doctor's office. He told me to go ahead, but he was sure it was nothing and he really didn't want to talk about it anymore. Fine. I called the special fertility office number. I talked to the nurse. She said that I would have to have a blood test. I was to go to the lab and have the blood drawn. The lab would send the results to them and I should know the results by the middle of the afternoon. I went. They drew. I waited. I tried to concentrate on work. Every time the phone rang, I jumped a little. I was nervous to pick up the phone wondering if the caller on the other end was the doctor's office. It never was.

Bill called about 4 to ask if I had heard anything yet. I hadn't. He told me to call them. This is 'Mr. I don't want to talk about it.' I called. They said they would call me right back. It was 4:55, the office closed at 5, when my phone rang. It was the nurse. Was I prepared for the disappointment? After all of these years, I should have been. I had also come to realize that I never was. There was always hope. The nurse told me who she was and they had the results. I will never forget her words: "You were right. You're pregnant!" After that, her questions became a blur. I didn't comprehend what she was asking me. I didn't know the answers to her questions. I just knew she told me I was pregnant. I was pregnant. I WAS PREGNANT! Bill called right at 5. He asked if I had talked to the nurse yet. I told him yes and we were pregnant. His response? "You're shittin' me!"

By the time I had gotten home, he had called his sister and a few other people. He was so excited! I was excited. I was scared. I had said I would take a miscarriage or any other sign that I could actually GET pregnant. Now, what would happen if that was the result? Could I actually survive that as well? I was very afraid, skeptical, nervous and any other emotion you can think of. We were finally here! What would happen if it all just went away in the blink of an eye?

I didn't want to tell too many people. I wanted to wait until that magical 12 week date. We went to my friend Julie's house. I worked with her husband, Kent, at a local TV station. He was in sales and I was the local traffic manager. Kent and Julie were two of our closest friends. I didn't want it out there for too many to know….just in case. We also went over to Tim and Vanessa's house and told them. Of course they were happy for us as well. Later Tim told me that Vanessa had cried when I left. He didn't understand why. I did. I tried to explain that you were happy for your friend and miserable for yourself. Unless you were a woman in that situation, it was hard to explain and define. (I should also mention that Vanessa went on to have 4 healthy children of her own.) With them being told, that was the limit of the people I wanted to tell.

The sales department had a meeting every Monday morning. Kent made the announcement. He told the entire sales staff. I guess my secret was out. Now, all we had to do was just sit back and see what happened.

I went to the doctor at 10 weeks. They couldn't hear the heartbeat, but it was still early. I was still pregnant. I was still scared. Tim's first wife, Connie, had gotten remarried and was pregnant with twins. She had lost them both at 14 weeks. I was at 10. There were no assurances or guarantees. I was still scared. At my 14 week appointment, there it was. The beautiful, loud sound like a washing machine, the baby's heartbeat was strong! It was the most exquisite sound I had ever heard! Now 22 years ago, they didn't just do routine ultrasounds on a baby. My doctor did not particularly care for them. They weren't sure if there would be any long term effects on the baby. There was talk about the sound waves doing damage to the hearing. He said I was fine and to see him in a month.

A little concrete proof would have been reassuring!

All that time, I was sick. I couldn't eat meat. The smell of cooking meat would make me sick. I couldn't even drive past a steak house or a Burger King. I could only eat lettuce and potatoes. I didn't care. If that was what it took, that was what I would do! I was constantly nauseous for the first 24 weeks. I didn't complain. It didn't matter. When I felt sick, it was a quick cracker or chip. It didn't stop it, it just lessened the nausea. I did crave that Dairy Queen sundae though. Chocolate soft serve with marshmallow topping was on my menu every night! It was either fortunate or unfortunate that we lived across the street from the Dairy Queen. I guess it depended on how you looked at it. The only thing that mattered was this baby. We didn't do the blood test for the possibility of Down's syndrome. We didn't want to know. Would it matter? We were at the point where there was going to be a baby at our house! The due date for the bundle of joy was November 21, 1993. This would be six and a half years since we got married and almost six since we started 'trying'. I guess that 11 month employee thing was going to be this year as well! With the baby due at the end of November, I would still be on maternity leave in December.

In September, I noticed that the ankle I had broken was really swollen. I was pregnant, wasn't it supposed to be a little bigger? The issue was that it was really starting to hurt. That part wasn't normal pregnancy issues. I decided that I should see the orthopedic doctor again. I made an appointment and went to see him. He looked at it. It was very swollen and red. I had an infection in that ankle. He said that my body may be rejecting the metal or I may have some kind of allergic reaction to it. He gave me some antibiotics to help with the infection. One that was also safe for the baby. It had better be! (I didn't find out until sometime later that if that infection had gotten worse and had gone to the bones, they would have had to amputate my foot!) That was taken care of and it was back to baby.

I didn't even start the baby's room until October. I was just so scared of something going wrong.

On November 14th, the doctor told me I had to quit work. My blood pressure was too high, 150/110. It usually ran extremely low. My normal was 90/60. There was protein in my urine. The only thing I was missing was the swelling. They were afraid of toxemia. I was to stay home with limited activity. OK, whatever you say, Doc. I agreed. I was not taking chances.

My parents came down for an early Thanksgiving. They just knew that when they were there, the baby would make its grand entrance. They went home. No baby.
November 21st came and went. We still didn't have a baby. At the doctor's appointment, I was told that if the baby did not come on its own, I would be induced on Monday, November 29th.

People said to make plans. A baby has a way of interrupting plans! We decided we would invite our friends, Marc and Wanda, to dinner on Saturday. It came with the understanding that plans could be cancelled on the spur of the moment. It would all depend on the baby's timing, not ours.

The baby trumps out!

Chapter 8

Three o'clock that Saturday afternoon, I got my first contraction. We called off dinner. At 7:00 p.m. we headed to the hospital. It had been 4 hours already. Those hours were spent lying on the couch and waiting to see if the contractions would continue. They did. When we got to the hospital, they hooked me up to monitors. We were there for a couple of hours. They sent us home. We were told I was in the early stages of labor. When it got worse, we were to come back. Oh, ok. What did that mean? We got home about 10 p.m. We decided to try and get some sleep. When you are 9 months pregnant plus a week overdue, sleep really wasn't an option. With that being said, we thought we should give it a try anyway. About 1:30 in the morning, the back labor started. It was intense. In Lamaze class they tell you it's uncomfortable. What they didn't tell you was that it was like a baseball bat hitting you in the lower back every 5 minutes. After each whack of the bat, the pain moved around to the front. I tried to let Bill sleep. I was screaming into my pillow. At 7 a.m., it was time to wake him up. I had been awake all night with this pain. He asked me why I didn't wake him up sooner. I told him I didn't know if it was bad enough yet. We decided we would go back to the hospital. We each took a shower. We got to the hospital about 8 a.m.

The nurse, Naomi, said we were the only ones there. It was her birthday and she could probably get out early. Sounded like a great plan to me! By noon, the contractions were so bad and no progress was being made. I was starting to fight the contractions. The medical staff strongly suggested I have an epidural. I agreed. The pain was still so intense that they upped the dosage. The epidural medicine had been so strong and in such big doses, I was completely numb from the waist down. I was numb and still not progressing much. They broke my water. With being a full week overdue, I should have had about a pound of water. I had closer to five pounds! That explained the no swelling and where that extra fluid went. There was still a lack of progression. Let's add Pitocin. Oh, ok. During labor, the baby would start and stop. Sometimes the contractions would be 8 minutes apart, go to 1 minute and the next one would be 5 minutes later. It was strange. There was no timing them. The contractions came and went with no rhythm or obvious progression. After hours and hours, I hit that magic 10 centimeter mark. Finally, the time had come to push. We had already been at the hospital for close to 10 hours. I was pushing by 5:45 p.m. Even with the pushing, it would start and stop. The doctor showed up around 6. The nurse told him we had variables. What the hell were variables?! With each push, my blood pressure would set off the alarm and the baby's would disappear. That couldn't be good! They let me continue on.

Shayla Rose O'Brien was born at 6:15 on Sunday night, November 28, 1993. She was 7 pounds 9 ounces and 21 inches long. 27 hours of hard labor. She was born with the cord wrapped around her arm and neck. Fortunately, it had not cut off circulation and breathing. She was fine. She was alive. She had these chubby cheeks, beautiful blue eyes and no hair. Words just couldn't describe the emotions of seeing our child for the first time.

She was beautiful.

Bill was calling people by 6:30. I talked to my parents. Why not? I could talk. I couldn't feel anything. Of course I couldn't walk either. Naomi, who thought she could go home early, was just going to fill out the paperwork at 8:00 that night. Sorry, Naomi.

No one told me about the post-delivery bleeding. Mine was horrible. But then again, it was my first. They didn't know my labor and delivery would be so unique…all the starting and stopping. Why should it be typical afterwards? I had bleeding for almost 3 weeks! I honestly didn't know that was out of the ordinary.

Everyone, every expert, every woman on the street tells you the best option was to breast feed your child. It was best for your child. Duh! But, what they didn't tell you was that sometimes you just couldn't! I was not prepared for that failure as well. Sometimes it was NOT an option. First of all, Shayla did not know how to eat. She had to be tube fed. The tube had to hit the back of her throat so she could learn how to suck. Not to be too disgusting here, but I don't know of anyone with 4 inch nipples! Now I am 'gifted' in the chest area. Here was another instance where size does not matter. The milk came in. The milk would not go out. Yes, these mammary glands that were big enough to satisfy a litter didn't work. Not only did they not work, it was painful! They got so engorged for no reason whatsoever!

So, you go with option two – bottles.

God bless Bill. He was actually excited about that. He wanted his turns feeding his daughter. He was looking forward to getting up in the middle of the night. Bill is a saint. He was definitely a hands-on dad. He was strutting around the hospital like he had done something no one had ever done before. He became a dad. He was so proud. His feet barely touched the ground.

It was the day to bring our baby home. I was more frightened by this prospect. I had never been around babies. Bill had been around them his whole life. Like I said, he comes from a family of 12. There were always nephews and nieces of all ages around his house while he was growing up. His mom babysat. How hard could it be? Change the diaper, feed the baby and put the baby to bed. Sleep when the baby does. Piece of cake.

That's what we heard. Don't believe everything you hear.

We took her home on Tuesday. That first night, it was time for my beautiful bundle to go to sleep. A few weeks earlier, we purchased a glider to put in the baby's room. I had visions of gently rocking my little one to sleep. I sat down in the glider with a bottle and my baby. I had her wrapped up in a blanket. We glided. She ate. She fell asleep. I put her in her crib. She cried. We started over. It was the same result. We tried again. It was the same result. I was exhausted. Maybe I can just hold her all night. No, that wouldn't work. What if I fell asleep and dropped the baby? We tried it again. Same result. Bill was sleeping. After all, he had to work in the morning and I wanted to do this! Next thing I knew it was 5 a.m. and I still hadn't gotten her to sleep! I could barely function! Let's try this: I wrapped her up in a blanket and set her upright in an infant seat. It worked! She stayed asleep. I went to our room for a bit of exhausted sleep.

It was short. She was not a sleeper.

Babies are supposed to be all cute and sleep a lot. No one told this to Shayla. She slept fitfully and for short amounts of time. She could hold her head up by the time she came home from the hospital. My baby was advanced - except for this whole sleeping thing. I remember my sister-in-law, Cheryl, coming over the day after we brought her home. She wanted to feed her. I gave her the bottle, but told her not to hold her lying flat. Shayla didn't like that. Cheryl held her flat. She looked at me and said, "Oh my God! She is trying to sit up!" The look on Cheryl's face was priceless. I told you she didn't like to lay flat!

Just a little over a week after bringing my baby-who-won't sleep home, she started throwing up. What the heck was this?! Now you may remember that I didn't know a lot about babies, but I did know their little bodies could get dehydrated pretty quickly. I didn't want that to happen. I decided I had better make a call to my doctor's office. We had a regular general practitioner that we saw and were going to take Shayla to see him. We made an appointment for later that morning. I took her in. She had a slight fever. There was another cause for alarm. Her heart rate was at 195 beats a minute! The doctor was quite concerned. That was frighteningly fast. She had the heart rate of a rabbit! Bill was a volunteer fireman and on the ambulance crew so the doctor allowed us to go home. He wanted Bill to check her heart rate at lunch. We were to bring her back later that afternoon. There was no change at noon. In the doctor's office that afternoon, it had risen slightly. The doctor was very concerned.

We were going to the hospital.

We took her to the neonatal intensive care unit because of her age. She was less than two a weeks old. They tested her. They put her in a little isolate. I cried. What was wrong? I just got her! This was Thursday. They kept her in the hospital until Saturday. I didn't leave. I couldn't leave. They decided that I couldn't take her home until I could prove that I knew how to do infant CPR. Are you kidding me?! Keep her! Make her better and then I would take her home. This was a nightmare. There was talk of a heart monitor, but that really only worked when the heart stopped. It was not designed for tachycardia (rapid heart rate). I proved that I could do CPR. I had been certified several times, so that was a bonus. We took our child home on Saturday afternoon. She would be fine. We just have to keep a close eye on her and see the doctor.

Guess again.

That night, Shayla started crying. We brought her into bed with us. She was turning blue and her chest was caving in. This was not good. We were scared. Bill said to get ready; we were taking her back to the hospital. It was back to the neonatal unit we went. She was admitted…again. Her heart rate was over 200. What the heck was going on?! I cried. Bill cried. It was just all too much. It took us so long to get her here. Was she going to leave us?

The next morning, three of Bill's sisters and a brother-in-law made the trip from Rochelle to Cedar Rapids. His sister, Kathy, was a nurse. I think Bill felt better with her there. Shayla's heart rate was at 235 beats per minute. Finally, we got what the problem was. Pneumonia. How did that even happen?

I have a theory. I may be way off, but it was what I believe. I told you that when they broke my water I should have had about a pound. They estimated I had about 5 pounds. Plus, during the delivery, during the pushing, she would start and stop. What I believe was that she ingested excess fluid at that time. Now this has not been proven. It's just my guess. It just took a week to develop into full pneumonia. I think part of human nature just wants an explanation. We all want to the answer to the all-important question of "Why?" This is the one I go with. It just makes sense to me. They deep suctioned her lungs and it brought her heart rate lower. She was getting better. On Tuesday we got to take her home again.

People are cruel.

Let me tell you this, people can be so insensitive. They have their own theories. "If you wouldn't have taken her out of the house, this wouldn't have happened." "If you would have breast fed, she wouldn't have gotten sick." Thank you. That makes me feel so much better. I am a horrible mother and I purposely did this to my child! People are dumb. I cried. I cried a lot. My child had just been in the hospital and we were horribly sleep deprived. Did people actually think I enjoyed this? Did they actually think that I would purposely put my child in harm's way? Did they actually think I would knowingly put my child in danger? Did they actually think they knew what they were talking about? People are insensitive idiots. Thank you for making me feel worse than I already did.

All of this actually made some sense as to why she hated to lay down. There must have been painful pressure in her head and chest. The pieces fit together. This was behind us. Now, we would have the chubby-cheeked, happy little bundle of joy. She would sleep. We would cuddle her, kiss her, enjoy her. This was what we waited 6 years for and worked so hard for. We had to have an EKG done a week after the hospitalization to check her heart rhythm. It showed such a radical difference from that last one that we had to have another. The second was much more acceptable. They assured us everything was good with her heart. The worst was behind us.

Or so we thought.

Beginning with the time of her first hospitalization, Shayla was sick all the time. I don't just mean a little cough or a runny nose. She was sick all the time. It started 12 days after she came home from the hospital. She was running a fever. Off to the doctor we went! She had an ear infection. Let's put her on some medicine. Oh, OK. This should work just fine. It did, for 10 days. Two days after the medication ran out, she was sick again. Back to the doctor we went because she was running a fever. She had an ear infection. Let's do more medicine. Sure, why don't we? We gave her the medicine for 10 days. On day 12 she was back at the doctor's office. She had an ear infection. Are you kidding me? This must be a really cruel joke!

It was no joke.

In the meantime, it was time to find daycare and time for this mom to go back to work. We found Donna. She had daycare out of her home. She was great. One problem down. I started back to work. You may think I'm a horrible mother. Why wouldn't I just stay home with this baby I worked so hard to get? It really wasn't an option. My work was fabulous at paying me my full salary for the 2 weeks I was off before she was born and for the six weeks of maternity leave. We needed my paycheck. Plus, as much as I loved and adored my child, I would not be a good stay-at-home mom. I am somewhat of a workaholic. It wouldn't be the best for both of us to be at home all day, every day. So back to work I went.

In February, my ankle started acting up again. The infection was back. I went back to the doctor. He told me my body really didn't like that metal. A surgery was scheduled to have it removed. It wasn't so bad. A couple of weeks in an air cast and I was good again.

Shayla was not.

Shayla still got sick. I'm serious when I say this; we had a standing doctor's appointment every 12 days. I would bring her in and on the way out we would set up the appointment because we knew she would be sick again. Why couldn't someone just stop it, for crying out loud! I will have to mention that I had the best boss ever! He was 54 when his only child was born and his wife was 37. He got it. He was very understanding about Shayla being sick and me having to miss work. I would have to call and say, "Shayla is sick again." He would tell me to take care of her and call him in the evening. Best boss award went to Dan!

We thought that maybe we should take her to a specialist. We saw an Ear, Nose and Throat doctor. It was decided that maybe putting tubes in her ears was the answer. Ok, let's do that! That would surely take care of all her problems. Have I mentioned that sleep came in hour or two intervals? Have I mentioned that every night…every night…at 8 p.m. she would start to cry? It could be 5 minute's worth of crying or two hours. We never knew. We just knew that at 8:00, we had better be home. We were. One night we were at Marc and Wanda's house. I looked at Bill and told him it was five minutes to 8. We both jumped up and said we had to go home. Right at 8, Shayla started crying. So, naïve as we were, we thought tubes were the answer. We scheduled the surgery.

This was very difficult. Taking our baby and handing her over to the nurse for surgery was hard. But, we thought this might be the answer to our prayers. Tubes would let her ears drain and lessen the frequency of infection. If not stop them, then maybe they wouldn't be so severe. It really was worth a try. The surgery was very quick and there were no complications. Finally! We had a solution to the problem. Shayla would stop these darn ear infections. We would cease with the standing doctor's appointments every 12 days. Finally, we would have our happy, healthy baby girl that we held in our dreams.

Guess what? Wrong again.

She continued to get sick. We continued to have the standing doctor's appointments every 12 days. The tubes really did nothing! Why couldn't someone just help us with this?! For six years we tried everything to get this baby here and she was sick, not just once, but all the time!

Let's add to the infections.

One Friday morning as I was changing her diaper, I noticed a spot on her cheek. I really didn't think much of it. Babies got little bumps like that all the time, right? I picked her up from the sitter that night. At 4 months old, Shayla had chicken pox! Yippee. The poor little thing. She did run a fever and have the scabs. She wanted to be held, but holding her made the pox worse. I would cuddle her for a while, but those spots needed to "breathe". We would put a garbage bag on the floor, cover it with a blanket, strip her naked, and lay her down. We gave her several oatmeal baths a day. I guess it was good in the fact that she couldn't scratch. After a few days, she seemed to get better. Disaster averted.

With all those doctor appointments and medications, there were highlights. In June, when she was 7 months old, we took a little trip. My dad used to pitch for the Brooklyn Dodgers Minor League baseball team. They were having a reunion in Ponca City, Oklahoma. We met my parents and spent a few days with them in Oklahoma.

From there, we continued south. We went to San Antonio, Texas. Shayla loved the water. Our hotel had a pool and she had a blast splashing around in it.

We did one of those river boat tours. We got off a little early because it was a very hot day and she was getting a little cranky. Bill wanted a glass of ice tea. We went into the first restaurant we came to. It was Hooter's. I didn't know what we were walking into. It was my first time ever in a Hooter's. I think Bill knew - the little trickster. I said we couldn't take a baby in there! He said it was a family restaurant and it was perfectly acceptable. I will say those waitresses loved Shayla. They swarmed our table. They asked if they could hold her. (We could see them the whole time.) They took her behind the bar. They brought her back – complete with lipstick stains on her bald head and a new "owl" shirt! She had the biggest smile! The guys at the table next to us said. "Next time we bring a baby!"

Shayla started walking at 9 months. She could see and hear. So developmentally she was OK. Thank God! She had chubby little cheeks and those beautiful blue eyes. She tried to be a happy toddler, but I think that was a difficult chore when, in your head, the pain was real and constant.

Because her birthday was around Thanksgiving, we celebrated her first birthday the first week in December. It was a great day. Our house was full of friends, family and neighbors. We went from not thinking we would ever have anything to celebrate to having a first birthday party. It was amazing! But, those infections just wouldn't leave my baby alone!

Not only did she still get sick, it got worse.

Chapter 9

One day in February, Bill and I were both at work. I was still working at a TV station in Cedar Rapids and Bill had a job in Hiawatha at New Outlooks (They did maintenance and sold supplies for commercial dishwashers and laundry machines.) Shayla was at the babysitter's house. I used to fill in at the switchboard so our receptionist could go to lunch. I answered the phone and it was Donna. She said she had just fed Shayla, but when she went to pick her up out of the highchair, she set her right back down. She was so hot. I needed to come and get her. I told her I would be there as soon as the receptionist returned. The receptionist came back from her lunch and I made arrangements to leave work early.

I went and picked her up at Donna's. When I got her home, I took her temperature. It was 102. I stripped off her sweatshirt, gave her some Tylenol and tried to get her to take a nap. That was the cure-all, right? She was down about 45 minutes. I'm not even sure she slept for any of that time. She was crying again. The temp was still 102. I called the doctor's office. The nurse, Mary, said to bring her in. While I was on the phone with the nurse, Shayla went into a grand mal seizure! Her entire body stiffened. She turned her head to the side. Her body violently shook. She foamed at the mouth. Her skin started to turn gray. I said, "Oh my God, Mary, she's having a seizure!" She said, "Call the ambulance!" I told her to hang up!

I called the ambulance and Bill. Since Bill was on the fire department, they came with every truck for 'one of their own'. It was horrible! I was crying hysterically. It was a good thing his work was so close. He got there pretty quickly! Bill came flying home from work and got there right after the ambulance. Our friend, Marc, the assistant chief, grabbed me and hugged me. They got oxygen on her and she was taken to the hospital. It was a febrile seizure (caused by fever). (To this day when I see Donna, she talks about how happy she was she made that call and Shayla didn't have the seizure with her!)

Let's NEVER do that again!

Well, wouldn't that have been a nice thought. The hours turned into days, turned into weeks. We survived. It was a schedule of work, a sick child, and doctor's appointments. Of course, people do look at you strangely when you say your child had a seizure, like you caused it or could have prevented it. They also gave you advice. Why did people who have never had to deal with anything close to what we were going through feel it necessary to give advice? Just like with the not being able to get pregnant, the breast-feeding, the ear infections. The advice was when she started getting a high temperature, run a bath. Make sure it was normal bath water temperature. Put her in it, then start cooling the water down. One night she was running a fever. We ran the bath water – normal bath temperature. We got her ready. We just barely dipped her toes in the water. She went into another seizure! She had the same symptoms as before. She was turning gray with blue lips. It scared the hell out of us! Her oxygen saturation was just so low during these 'episodes'.

Another ambulance call. Another ear infection. Damn it!

Needless to say, we were becoming way past the point of exhaustion and frustration. My job at the TV station had me working long hours for little pay. Bill was taking Shayla to daycare, picking her up and spending time with her all while I was at work. She was such a Daddy's girl. It actually broke my heart a little bit. Who am I kidding, it was devastating. Bill was not really satisfied with his job. He wasn't really sure what he wanted to do, but New Outlooks wasn't it. We had always talked about moving to Whittemore when we retired for the slow-paced, small town living. We talked about it and decided to make the move sooner rather than later. We made the trip to Whittemore to look for a house and a job. We decided to purchase my grandparents old home. I loved this house. It had 5 bedrooms, 2 bathrooms, built in 1912 with all the gorgeous woodwork, windows, porches, big rooms and walk-in closets. It was only a half a block away from my parents.

Bill got a job with Algona Vault Service and I got a job at Pharmacist Mutual Insurance Company. Our house was in Whittemore, but our jobs were in Algona. It was a 10 mile drive from one to the other. It was all coming together. We would begin our new jobs in the middle of March 1995. Shayla was about 17 months old. We put our house on the market and it sold in 4 days. However, the people who currently owned the house we had purchased needed to find a place. It would be 6 weeks before we could move into our new home. We coordinated possession dates with all three parties – including the people who bought our home in Hiawatha. Our jobs started in 2 weeks and we moved in with my parents temporarily. We decided to move some things to Whittemore, but not everything. There was no place to put it. We would go back and forth on weekends and take our time to pack.

Living with my parents had its good points and not-so-good points. My wonderful, beautiful mother had dinner ready for us after work. Our laundry was done. Shayla refused to sleep. She would sleep about 20 minutes at a time. That is no exaggeration. She refused to sleep in the crib. We had to have her in bed with us. It did not make easy nights for us or my parents. Shayla's refusal to sleep affected everyone in the house. Now let me tell you this, I was not cut out for insurance work. To me, it was mind-numbingly boring. With getting no sleep, this was a bad combination. We struggled through the work week. Shayla was still getting sick. We were still seeing doctors.

One weekend we went back to Hiawatha to work on packing up the house. We were packing room by room. My friend, Julie, and I planned to take a little break and do some quick shopping. Bill and Shayla were going to stay at home. Now remember, this was a time before everyone had a cell phone attached to them at all times. We were gone for a few hours. When we got back, Bill told me Shayla had another seizure. They had already been to the hospital and back. She had another ear infection. Talk about GUILT! I couldn't believe I was out shopping while my poor baby was sick! I was sick!

Since they were released from the hospital and at home, we decided we would continue packing. We tried to organize and work a little here and a little there. Later that afternoon, Shayla toddled off into the kitchen. She was staring out the patio doors from across the room. She screamed. I looked out the door. I didn't see anything. I looked at her as she collapsed into my arms. She went into another seizure! Second one of the day! We called the ambulance. They took her away again. The doctor told us that two seizures in one day got her a stay in the hospital. What was the culprit causing the seizures? Ear infection.

Who would be the one to make this stop?!

We stayed at the hospital that night. The doctor came in at 5:00 p.m. on Sunday and said we could take her home. She still had a fever of 104. She had 2 seizures the day before. The doctor told us not to worry, she wouldn't have any more. But she had TWO yesterday! We took her home. She had her meds. (By this time, she has had so many rounds of medicine; she was becoming immune to quite a few!) We packed up the things we needed and began the 4 hour drive back home. Many, many times on the way home, we stopped, we turned on the dome light, and we checked her. We didn't want another seizure in the car. We had to work tomorrow! My mom kept Shayla the next day so I could go to work. To be honest, I got to work in the morning but I couldn't function. I broke down in tears to my boss. I ended up going home. I just couldn't do it.

We got through the next week and a half. Then, about day 12, she was sick again. Of course she was! I took her to the doctor. We told the doctor about Shayla's history. He didn't think a seizure was anything to worry about. He gave us a prescription and told us to give it to her when she started getting sick and continue until 2 days after her symptoms were gone. It was refillable. Finally! We could stop with the frequent trips to the doctor and fill a prescription as needed. That night, she was crying and the temp was going up. Bill went to get the medicine. We had a hard time getting her to take it. I'm sure the taste was awful, I know the smell was! We got about half a dose down and waited a little bit.

What happened next scared the crap out of both of us.

She became lethargic. She just had this blank open-eyed stare. She looked like she had died. It was horrible! We were up with her all night. What the heck just happened? Was it a horrible reaction to this miracle drug? What we found out the next day infuriated us. It was no miracle drug, it was Valium! They gave us the generic form, so I didn't even think to ask! I will say I was pretty naïve and trusting of the doctors. They went through all that schooling. They knew more than I did. We were pissed! Bill took the medicine and flushed it down the toilet. She was never getting that again. Our trust was shattered.

Bill had had it!

He called Mayo Clinic in Rochester, Minnesota. It was now time to go to the big dogs! We were able to make the appointment ourselves without a referral and we went. Our appointment was in May. Shayla was now 18 months old. She wasn't sleeping through the night and neither were we. As I think back on it, I don't know how we all survived with so little sleep.

What we really liked about Mayo was that it was all about you. The doctors put enough time aside to devote their consultation visit just for you! Finally, someone was there to listen! We told the doctor about the seizures. We told him how the doctor back home said they were no big deal and they wouldn't hurt her. His response was that they hadn't hurt her yet, but that didn't mean the next one wouldn't. We needed to get these to stop. Her body was doing one thing and the brain was doing another and one of them had to give.

We also told him that I have a brother and a nephew with epilepsy. That was a fact that all the other doctors seemed to have discounted. We really needed to see if there was a correlation. He also said that most children would have no seizures. Some children may have 1. But if she has already had 4, the likelihood was pretty high that she would have more. He scheduled us for more tests. He gave us some medicine. It sure as hell wasn't Valium! When we told him about that, he was appalled. Why would you put a child on Valium! The new medicine was Phenobarbital. We were to give her a dose every day. Now this sounded better already! He did examine her. We asked about tonsils. He said that they couldn't take her tonsils out. She had to have tonsillitis 4 times within 12 months in order to do that surgery. We were going to look at other options first.

We scheduled an appointment to have an EEG done. On the day of the test, Bill had to work. My mom and I were going to take her. We headed off to Rochester at 4:30 in the morning. She had to have an EEG done while she was awake and one while she was sleeping. By the way, she was over a year and a half old and still not sleeping through the night. The awake one wasn't so bad. Then we had to give her some medicine to help her fall asleep. As we sat there with her in the room waiting for her to fall asleep, the nurse came in. The nurse asked how I was doing. I said I was fine, but Shayla was not about to fall asleep. She asked my mom how she was doing. My mom said not so good and burst into tears. I guess until that moment I didn't know how worried and upset all this was making others as well. It seemed like it was entirely our problem. We were so frustrated. We were so tired. We were so worried. So were others that were close to us. We were at the end of our ropes. Shayla never did give up and fall asleep. We had to skip that one test.

We headed back towards home. Shayla fell asleep the minute we put her in her car seat. That little stinker! It was a 2 ½ hour drive. We were exhausted. Driving through a small town in Minnesota, I got my first speeding ticket ever! Talk about adding insult to injury. Thanks, Officer. I took my ticket and went home.

There was more to add to the dilemma.

Chapter 10

We had been in Whittemore about 3 months. It was June 1995. We were in our new home. Shayla had a daycare provider. (I'm surprised anyone would take her with her history.) There was one time when I went to pick her up and the babysitter had her outside stripped to her diaper. She said she felt warm and didn't want to take any chances. That was comforting. We knew the sitter would watch her and make sure she was as 'safe' as possible. We had settled into our jobs. I still hated mine. I told Bill that maybe I could get a part-time job at the radio station in town. At least I would be doing something I liked. Plus, the extra money wouldn't hurt. I got a job doing weekend shifts and operating the board during sports broadcasts at the radio station. I realized that once again I was 'late'.

Pregnant? Me with no drugs?

I took the home test. It showed a faint sign of positive. Gulp! We had only been at our jobs for a couple of months! I made an appointment to have the blood test done. I got the results. It was positive. I couldn't believe this actually happened! We were a little shocked, but also happy. We didn't have a repeat and years of infertility. We had a miracle! Even though we were excited, we were anxious. I remember when I told my parents and they weren't too happy. I think they were worried about our jobs. I was too. I would be at mine a little over a year the time the baby was due. That date was March 21, 1996. It took us 6 years last time. This time we didn't even try! Frightened or not, I was going to embrace this and thank God He gave us this miracle. My sister-in-law, Twila, was also pregnant. She was due March 22. It was going to be great! Babies everywhere!

Because we were living in Whittemore, we went to a doctor in Emmetsburg. He was a general practitioner. The nearest OB was an hour away. We decided I would just go to the GP. Others I knew had gone to him and were happy. This would work just fine for us. We had an appointment. Everything seemed to be going well.

I had never really thought much of intuition until that time. I just couldn't believe I was pregnant without really trying. After everything we had gone through, I don't think the 'trying' ever really stopped subconsciously. However, there was this little voice in the back of my head telling me all was not good. I tried to talk to Bill about it. I told him I just couldn't seem to shake the feeling that something was wrong. We both tried to assure ourselves that I was just being scared and a little paranoid. After you had a 'healthy' baby, the chances were pretty high that your next one would be also.

I went to doctor's appointments. The heartbeat was there. I was not gaining weight, but it was still pretty early. I was at week 20 and still had no need for maternity clothes. My head was thinking that was good. There would be less weight to lose! I was also thinking I should be gaining some weight. I told him of the labor and delivery with Shayla; how it would start and stop. I also told him about the cord being wrapped around her arm and neck. He decided that I should have an ultrasound in a couple of weeks. This was new. This was exciting. OK, let's do that! Having an ultrasound would surely give me the confirmation I needed. No matter how hard I tried, I just couldn't shake that voice in the back of my mind telling me that everything was *not* fine.

There was some movement from the baby, but it was painful and deep on the right side. Maybe I was just imagining this. We would have the ultrasound and then I would be able to relax and enjoy the rest of the pregnancy. We could get ready for our surprise addition. It would be awesome! I tried to be excited about it. I did worry a little about the whole job thing, but then I just didn't care. We wanted this baby. We were excited for this baby. Somehow everything would be just fine.

Meanwhile, Shayla was walking, running, and loves anything with music. She was talking. We used to tell her things were pretty and not to touch. She wouldn't touch anything we deemed as pretty. Her first word was pretty. She was constantly at her Daddy's side. We asked her if we should have another baby at our house. Her answer was "No!" We just thought we'd bring that subject up later.

The ultrasound was scheduled for November 1st at 1:30 in the afternoon. If you remember, this is also the anniversary of our first date! How ironic! Bill couldn't get off work to go with me. I could do this by myself. I did tease him, though. I told him I was going to find out the sex of the baby and not tell him. That was the price he had to pay for not coming with me.

I got to the hospital, which was right across the street from the doctor's office. The ultrasound began. This should take about 15 minutes. He was looking and looking. He slid that mouse-thing all over my stomach. He did that for about an hour! He said that he needed to do a baseline probe. Yep, that one was internal. He was having a hard time getting a good picture of the baby. The baby was buried deep to one side. That explained the pains. Another hour went by. He apologized to me that it was taking so long. I said it was OK as long as the baby was alright.

What he said to me next made the world stop.

Chapter 11

"I can't tell you that."

He asked when I had my next doctor's appointment. I told him at 4. Yes, I was going to be late. He told me to go ahead and get dressed and go over to my appointment. He would talk to the doctor and let him know what he found.

I started crying. What do you mean everything was not alright! I went across the street. I was crying. They took me as the last patient of the day. Yes, I sat in the waiting room for over an hour crying knowing something was wrong. Finally, they called my name and I went to the back.

The doctor walked in. The next words spoken to me will forever be etched in my mind. He had his hand to mid-forehead and swipes it back over the top of his head. He said, "From here back your baby has no skull. The second it is born it is going to die. What do you want to do?" No emotion. No sympathy. Cold. Hard. Matter of fact. How the hell should I know? Then he said to decide if I wanted to go to Mayo, Iowa City or Sioux Falls, South Dakota. You just pulled the rug out from under me. You just sent my world crashing and you want an immediate answer? I told him I would call him in the morning. I cried and cried and cried. I walked like a zombie to my car. I then realized I had forgotten my prescription. I went back in. They had a little pharmacy in the doctor's office. I gave the pharmacist the prescription. He looked at my face and asked if I was okay. I couldn't speak. At least HE had some sympathy! He gave me this sad face and went to get me the medicine.

The drive home was 15 miles. It was dark. I cried pretty hysterically the entire way home. I don't know how I kept from going off the road or running into someone else. Like

I said, these were the days before cell phones. Bill was at home. He had no idea what had just happened.

Somehow, I did make it home safely.

We had 5 steps from the mud porch up into the kitchen. I opened the door into the kitchen and literally fell into the house sobbing. Bill was on the phone. He said he had to call them back - whoever it was. Between sobs I told him that the baby was going to die. He called my parents and they came running right over. I told them that the baby had 0% chance of survival. The second it was born, it would die. We needed to decide where to go for this second opinion. Frankly, I don't remember much of that night. I do remember that I wanted to climb to the roof of our big house and jump off. Why bother? It just seemed as though I was a failure at everything! I couldn't get pregnant. I finally did have the baby we so longed for and she was sick all the time. I got pregnant again and the baby would die. This was the second time I wished I would have had a miscarriage. It would have been painful and devastating; however I wouldn't have had to go through all the harsh words and decisions. It would have been over. I know that's not fair. If the baby has 0% chance of survival, why was I allowed to carry it? Again, this was not in any means meant to be cruel and heartless for anyone who has suffered a miscarriage. This was where my brain was; what was going through my head. This couldn't be really happening to us.

It was.

We decided that because we used to live in Cedar Rapids, we would go to Iowa City. We still had friends there and my brother, Steve, and my sister-in-law, Cheryl, didn't live far away. Somehow we got through the night. I made the call in the morning to say that we would go to Iowa City. I called in sick to work. I stayed at home and cried all day. I couldn't stop it. You would think that your tears would eventually run out. They don't.

My mom had talked to our pastor. He came over to visit that day. He told me that his wife had to have her cervix sewn closed and complete bed rest because she was in danger of delivering too early. I looked at him and said that if it would make a difference, I would do it. I would stand on my head for a month. I would eat grass. I would walk across fire. Nothing could change this. Nothing was going to help. NOTHING! Don't you get it? This baby was going to die. Period.

In between fits of hysteria, I would think that maybe, just maybe, they were wrong. Maybe our baby would live but have a handicap. That wouldn't be what anyone would wish for, but at least we would still have our child. OK. Let's see…we have a bedroom down on the main level. That would work. We would have to build a ramp up to the kitchen. The mud porch was big enough. That would work. Was the bathroom door wide enough to get a wheelchair in? We didn't need to worry about that until the baby was a few years old. Our baby may be handicapped, but it was ours. They were wrong. WRONG! This was not happening. It would not die!

I got a call from the doctor. The appointment was set for November 4th.

We made the trip toward Iowa City. The four hour drive was filled with fear and maybe just a touch of hope. The guy in Emmetsburg was wrong. It was a small town. They had bigger and better things at the University of Iowa Hospitals. They would see that and the baby would live. We would have struggles, but we were in this and there would be a baby at our house. We stayed at my brother and sister-in-law's house.

The next day we went to the University of Iowa Hospital. I was a nervous wreck when we pulled into that parking lot. We went into the hospital and made our way to the appointment.

I was taken to the room for an ultrasound. In the next few minutes, the world came crashing in on me again. They were right in Emmetsburg. The baby did not have a skull. The baby had spina bifida. The baby had a club foot. The baby will die, if not before, when it is born. Because of the position of the baby, they couldn't even determine the gender. What did we want to do? I wanted to have a C-section. That couldn't be done. If I were to have a C-section when the baby was that small, the chances of carrying a full term baby in the future were slim. Did I want to be wheeled into delivery immediately? Did I want to wait until I delivered naturally? What did I want to do? I wanted this to be a bad dream, that was what I wanted! Oh, and there was one more thing. Without the skull, the amniotic fluid was deteriorating the brain. That was causing toxic fluids into my blood stream. Not only will this baby die, but I could also get very sick. What did we want to do?

Bill went to a pay phone and called his family. I was crying with my sister-in-law in the same hallway. Bill just broke down. He later told me that he didn't break down when he initially found out about the baby. He had to be the man. He had to be tough and take charge. After the confirmation at U of I Hospitals, he broke down into tears. He was absolutely every bit as heartbroken as I was. He just didn't want me to see it. I told him he didn't have to hide emotions from me. He didn't always have to be tough. We were in this together.

We decided to go home and make a decision.

On the way home, we talked about it. What was there really to talk about? Bill said he just lost his child; he couldn't lose his wife too. We decided to go back to Iowa City to have the baby.

We went home and called the next day. We also made an appointment with the funeral home. Bill, my parents and I went to meet with the funeral home. I had to pick out a tiny casket. This was just so wrong! What did we want on the bulletins? What was the baby's name? What kind of service? What day? STOP!!! How the hell should I know? I couldn't even function! We should be picking out colors for the baby's room, not cemetery plots and caskets!

We named the baby Kelly Lynn. We weren't sure of the gender, so we went with a name that would work for a boy or girl. The funeral would be on Saturday, November 11th. Veteran's Day. It was a long, holiday weekend. That way, Bill's family might have a chance to attend if they wanted to. I chose a small white casket. I had to pick out a tombstone and buy a cemetery plot! My head was screaming that this should NOT have been happening! But it was. The tombstone had a baby angel with its arms around a little lamb in one corner and a rose bud in the opposite. The hospital gave us a pamphlet that read, "To Us You Will Exist. In the flowers, in the trees and all thing of nature. You are now in a world of peace and happiness forever." I wanted this on the back of the tombstone. The funeral service would be graveside only.

That was done. I cried.

We went back to Iowa City. From the time of the ultrasound confirmation until we went back to Iowa City, Kelly had died in utero. I delivered our daughter. Because of the condition of her head, we chose not to see her. The nurse offered us an ultrasound picture of her arm. We took that. (Bill kept that ultrasound picture in his wallet for years.)

She had Trisomy 18. It's an extra #18 chromosome. It was a severe case. Trisomy 18 is a pretty devastating birth defect – only about 10% survive – most are stillborn. Children who did survive were developmentally smaller and cannot survive on their own. A distended abdomen does not let the heart and lungs develop fully and most cannot take a breath outside the womb. But this is just one of the characteristics of Trisomy 18. Most are dreadful and most are fatal.

My parents also went with us to Iowa City. The delivery didn't take long. Afterwards, I was taken to a room. My mom was waiting for me. She held my hand. We both just cried.

They asked if we would participate in medical research. If it could help someone else, why not!? If just one person could be saved from this heartache, we were in. We both got a cheek swab. That was it. We were done.

Our daughter was placed in a box wrapped in brown paper. We placed this box in the back of our car. We went back to Whittemore. We dropped her off at the funeral home on our way by. It was by far the very worst day of my life; November 7, 1995.

A few of Bill's family came in for the funeral. It was just a graveside committal. Pastor read the quote that is on the back of her headstone. It was just a nightmare, right. Any moment, I was sure I would wake up from this and we would have our baby girl, blonde hair and blue eyes, on our laps. THAT was what was supposed to happen. I was not to be buying plots and a casket. But it did happen. I think I was numb. I really don't remember a lot except feeling empty.   I robotically went through the day. I did remember Bill sitting graveside and he was crying. Shayla, our sweet, blue-eyed baby, says "Why is Daddy crying?" It just broke my heart. Bill waited until everyone was gone and lowered her into the grave. He wanted to be the one to lay her to rest. It was his way of saying good-bye. We went to the church for a lunch. The rest of that day was a blur.

I remember Bill's mom and sister, Mary, stayed at the house. They were going to be leaving the next day. We did get through that night.

Maybe, in time, I could function normally again. Reality hit us the very next morning.

Chapter 12

They have said, "God will never give you more than you can handle". I didn't know who 'they' were. Have 'they' ever been in this situation? I doubt it. I really didn't think I could handle one more thing. I thought I had reached my limit. We both had. We just wanted a happy marriage, a house with a white picket fence and a couple of kids playing in the yard. We had handled more than our share.

At least that's what we thought.

At 6:00 a.m. the following morning, we were awakened by Shayla. She was having a seizure! We had people at our house! We had just buried a daughter! This couldn't even be happening! But it was. Shayla was convulsing. She was turning gray. The ambulance was called. She was off to the hospital. They told us it was pneumonia and she spent the night in the hospital. She went home the next day.

I hadn't been at my job very long and didn't really have time off. But seriously, this was a not an everyday occurrence. I had to go to work on Tuesday. Somehow I mechanically made it through that day. Wednesday I think I pretty much cried all day. On Thursday, I was called into the HR office. The HR director asked me what days I was gone so she could 'dock me the right amount of days'. I was only allowed 3 days for sick leave. Sure. Let's call it sick leave. Let's not call it maternity. Let's not call it bereavement. I was just sick. Yes, I WAS sick. I was sick of the trials and tribulations. I was sick of running my daughter to the doctor and hospital. I was sick that I just buried my child. Why not kick me even harder? No feeling. No sympathy. I will never forget it. Even if that's what you thought, would it be that hard to be kind and feeling. It seemed so. HR stands for Human Relations. Maybe she needed a course in how to relate to humans! I was rather furious about that encounter.

Let's also add in the salesman who asked me how Kelly died. I told him. He said it was Ok that she died because she was going to have issues anyway. Are you kidding me? There are people whose children have handicaps. I'll bet if you asked them, they wouldn't wish this was the outcome! I would have put in the ramps. I would have done whatever it took to make her as happy as possible. This guy's wife had died of cancer. Would I ever have said it was OK that she died because she was sick anyway? NEVER! I wanted this baby. Even though she never took a breath, she was my daughter. She was loved. She was wanted.

I said I would take any sign that I could get pregnant. I got what I wished for. I should have been more specific.

There is not a day goes by that I don't think of the possibilities. We always picture her as a blonde-haired, blue-eyed little girl. I think of her as healthy and running around in heaven with friends and family that have gone on before her or have joined her afterwards.

Kelly Lynn O'Brien, you are loved.

Chapter 13

At the end of the month was Shayla's second birthday. We celebrated with family at our house. She was growing up so quickly, but still there were no answers as to why she was sick all the time.

In December, we decided to make the 7 hour drive to Rochelle to see Bill's family for Christmas. Bill's sister, Mary, and her husband J.P., loved to spoil Shayla. I had mentioned that we needed to get a Christmas dress for Shayla, so off to Rockford we went for a little shopping trip. We found a beautiful, purple velvet dress that they insisted on buying for her. They also bought her a winter coat. I mentioned that I needed to stop at Walmart for some tights. (They bought those too, but not at Walmart.) It was a fun shopping day and Shayla was a little trooper. She was getting tired, though, and it was time to head back for a nap.

When we got there, she was very restless. Bill tried lying with her to see if she would go to sleep. She didn't sleep much, but in a strange place it was even more difficult. He had enough and it was my turn to lay with her. The back bedroom was pretty dark. Bill checked on us to see how it was going. I told him to turn on the light. Something just didn't seem right. Shayla was having a seizure! We made yet another call for an ambulance.

I have said before that Bill comes from a family of 12 kids. This was the first ambulance visit to their house. His sister, who didn't live too far away, called his mom to see where the ambulance was going. She said "Here!" Any guesses as to what was wrong with Shayla? She had an ear infection and a fever of 102. Bill's sister, Kathy, was a nurse at the hospital so she met us there. We stayed at the hospital for a time to make sure she was stable. They gave us some medication and we went back to Bill's parent's house. We called Mary and J.P. and told them what just happened. They were in shock. She was perfectly fine! There was our frustration. It came so quickly. This was seizure #6.

Tears of worry. Tears of frustration. How much more could her little body take?

We got through Christmas. She was on medicine. She was still sick all the time. She was over 2 years old and still didn't sleep through the night. We were so far past exhausted. It was hard to say how much more we could take. What were we supposed to do now?

One day, I was coming home from work and walking into the house. There was a little dip in the sidewalk that had ice hiding under a fine layer of snow. I fell. My ankle HURT! I waited until Bill got home. We decided to have it checked out at the hospital. When we got there, the ER nurses look at my foot, pointed to a spot and said it really looked like it was broken. Again?! They took x-rays. I was told the break looked like an old one. Wait just a minute! I had never broken it in that spot before! I believed them and off we went. I was still a little confused about the break/no break diagnosis, but believe it or not, I still trusted doctors.

Since we were told there was no problem with my foot, we had to figure out how to make Shayla better. We decided that she was going to see and Ear, Nose and Throat doctor in Mason City. Why not? We had been to so many already, what was one more doctor? We thought we would try this. Maybe he would be the one to help Shayla. We made an appointment in April. The doctor said that he was going to take her tonsils out. They were quite large. We were told previously that if she didn't have tonsillitis 4 times in 12 months they wouldn't do it. This doctor said he would.

It was June of 1996. Shayla was going in for her second surgery. I was hopeful. I was apprehensive. I was scared. I wanted this to work. I wanted this to be the answer. The surgery was very quick. By the time I picked up a magazine in the waiting room, she was done. The doctor told us she had "caverns filled with chronic infection on the back side of her tonsils". That made sense. The infection 'hid' while she was on medication. It came back out 2 days after the medication was done. The infection never really left – ever.

This would do the trick!

She came through the surgery just fine. Wouldn't you know it; there was a little hitch in the recovery. She wouldn't swallow. She wouldn't drink. The next day I just followed her around with a washcloth. She wouldn't even swallow her own saliva. That next night as we were getting her ready for bed, we changed her diaper. It was dry. I asked Bill if he had changed her. He hadn't. I hadn't. She was in the same diaper all day and it was dry. In the morning, it was a little wet. It was very foul smelling and a brownish color. We called the doctor's office. We were told to get her to the hospital. We took her to Mason City. She was put in the hospital and on an i.v. for fluids. She was dangerously close to dehydration. They said a 24 plug-in would do her some good. That night, she kept asking for cheese. The nurses named her Miss Mouse. By the morning, she was eating and drinking. I will never forget her breakfast. She took Honey Nut Cheerios and dipped them in butter. Not what I would want for breakfast, but at least she was eating.

Now that was the ticket!

After her surgery, she didn't get sick any more. She was almost impossible to get to sleep, but once she did, she stayed asleep. After 2 ½ years, and a few months after her surgery, she was finally sleeping through the night!

FINALLY!

Chapter 14

It was early summer. My foot still really hurt after that second fall on the ice. We decided that maybe I should see a different doctor. I made an appointment in Spencer. The doctor there did a bone scan. He told me there was good news and bad news. Let's have the bad and end with the good. I had bone chips that were jammed into my joint. They should probably be surgically removed and clean up the scar tissue in my ankle. Yippee. Ankle surgery number 3. The good news? He told me my break was almost healed! So the break they told me was an old one, wasn't. It was broken and I had been walking on a broken foot for 6 months! No wonder it hurt! The surgery was scheduled. It was done and there were no complications. It was time to move on.

One day that summer, my sister-in-law, Twila, was going to take her kids swimming at the city pool. (She had baby Jonathan in March, just like she was supposed to.) She had 4 kids, plus Jonathan. She couldn't watch all those kids plus a baby. I told her I would watch Jonathan while she took the others to the pool. She asked if I was sure. Yeah, I was sure. Why wouldn't I be? Sitting alone with Jonathan, it hit me. I should have one the same age. They should be friends and they could be playing together right now, except mine was in the cemetery. I just hugged Jonathan and cried.

Now that Shayla was actually better, I wanted to move forward. I didn't know if I was a glutton for punishment or what, but it was time to talk about another baby. After Kelly had died, I wanted to start trying the next month. Bill was the one who suggested we wait. With all the issues we had on our plate with Shayla, he thought that maybe we should tuck this plan away temporarily. But, I was 35 years old! You weren't supposed to have babies after you were 35. There was a greater risk and all that business. We had already had enough. Was I just tempting fate?

Fate wasn't what I was tempting, it was Bill.

A few months had gone by. He really didn't say much about it. He was pretty much silent about it. To have a baby, you had to have a schedule, at least in our world you did. Timing was everything. Well, he was not cooperating. Finally, it just came to a boil. We had a pretty heated discussion. I wanted a baby. He did not. He was scared. I was scared. Look at all we had been through in the last 9 years! He said he was petrified that we would have another Kelly. I was afraid of that also. I just looked at him and said I did not want an only child. Did he? If people wanted to have only one, that was their right. It was not what I wanted. I looked at him and said if anything would happen to Shayla, we would have no one. If anything happened to us, she would have no one. I didn't want to put her through that. He asked what would happen if we had another baby like Kelly. I told him that we had been through it already. We could deal with it – not easily, but we could handle it. If that was what happened again, we would be done. He reluctantly agreed to try.

It was time to see doctors again. When I thought about it, did I really want to go through this all over again? I had been very unsuccessful in the children department. One took 6 years to get here and then was sick all the time. The second one died before she had a chance to live. Was I really pushing my luck too far? What could possibly happen that hadn't already happened to us? With our history, I should never ask that question. I am human. That question was very real and I'm not sure if I wanted to know the answer.

I had a doctor's appointment with my doctor in Mason City. Because of my age and history, I was a high risk candidate. I went to my appointment. The doctor wanted me to do a temperature chart. Oh goodie. That was such an exciting thing for me. I think I could wallpaper my house with temperature charts! As this was his first time working with me, he wanted to see what he was dealing with. OK, fine. Let's just do this.

I took the chart and went on my merry way.

It was back to taking the temperature before my feet hit the floor in the morning. Yay. Mark that down. Day after day. After the month was over, I went back to the doctor. Yes, I had a spike in my temperature so that was good. In order not to waste time, the doctor suggests that I go on Clomid. Wait just a minute here! I could go on and on with my horror story about Clomid! Cysts. Surgeries. Pain. Was I willing to take that risk? Why would he even suggest it? Did I have a choice? How bad did I really want this? Was I willing to go through all of that again? Should I? The answer was simple. Yes. The doctor believed it was the right plan of action. Here we go again! We were going back to the unknown and the risks.

I got my prescription and I took it at the appropriate time. I had my chart. I was praying that this wasn't another 6 year 'project'. I didn't have that much time! Let me tell you, Bill was as sick of schedules and charts just as much as I was. There was nothing like sex on a schedule. It really took the mood right out of what you had to do.

I marked my chart. On day 14, my temperature went up. We knew what that meant. Let's get down to business. It was more like business. It was not fun. It was not spontaneous. It was not romantic. It was simply a way to a result. Bill didn't really want to on the night we HAD to! Yeah, I was pissed. Since he was kind of important in this whole process, what now? We fought. That was really not the answer I was looking for. However, I did understand it. This had been difficult on our marriage. It hadn't been just a month or two. It had been years of schedules and having to 'perform' when the charts say so. I don't think it was what either of us really signed on for. This was what we were dealt. We were still together. We were still a family. But with everything that had happened in the last nine years, it hadn't been easy.

Two days later, he wanted to do this. Great, Bill, we just missed it. I have a doctor's appointment in a couple of weeks. I can just tell him my husband wasn't in the mood. I continued my chart. My temperature didn't go down. It would. I just knew it would. We should have tried on day 14, not day 16. Once again, we will be back to where we were before.

I had my doctor's appointment. The first thing he asked was to look at my chart. He looked at it and said, "You're pregnant." Slow down here, Doc. I mean, "YAY!", but slow down. I looked at him and asked how he knew for sure. He said my temperature didn't go down. That's it? Your whole basis for that announcement was my stupid temperature chart? He asked if I wanted to take a pregnancy test. Sure, Doc, humor me. I took the urine test. It was negative. See, I told you! I told the nurse that the doctor said I was pregnant. She asked if I want to do a blood test. Humor me. Yes. Since my appointment was at the end of the day, I would have to wait until tomorrow for the results. I said that would work. I had an hour drive back home and I wanted to stop at a store on the way. I thanked them and said we would talk again tomorrow.

I stopped at Kmart in Mason City. Again, this was in the day of no cell phones. I had a calling card. I called home to let Bill know that I stopped at the store and would be heading home in a few minutes. I told him I was late getting on the road because the doctor's appointment had taken longer than I had originally thought. He said that was understandable because I was pregnant. What did you just say? He said the doctor had called our house and told him that the blood test was positive and we were expecting another baby! It was odd, though, that he knew for sure before I did. The doctor later apologized for that. Some women didn't want their husbands to know. I wasn't upset, I was ecstatic!

Now that I had that news, the worry didn't go away. Look at our track record. Would this be a repeat Kelly? We prayed that it wasn't. Until we got the official word, that thought would always be in the back of our minds. We told my parents we were expecting again. They, again, were not happy. I think they were just as scared as we were. We needed reassurance.

I had a doctor's appointment in my tenth week. I went into the doctor's office. They tried to get the baby's heartbeat. It couldn't be detected. Panic? You could call it that. He scheduled an ultrasound for the next day.

Bill couldn't get off work. Even though my work wasn't very happy with the time I had to take off, I didn't really care. I scheduled all my appointments for as late in the day as possible and made up my hours. Let's just say that being an insurance underwriter technician wasn't exactly an exciting, demanding or stressful job. It was mind-numbingly boring. Most days I wondered how to get through the day awake. It was a job with benefits. (I still didn't like the job and they were not so understanding when Kelly died. That being said, I gave them my best when I was at work. It didn't mean I loved it. It meant they paid me to work and do my best, and that's what they got. They just didn't get my love.)

Since Bill couldn't go to the ultrasound, I took my Mom with me. It didn't even hit me that she had never been to or seen an ultrasound before. The technician did her job. She found the baby. We heard the heartbeat. My mom had tears in her eyes. I was relieved. She couldn't believe how small the baby was. It looked a lot bigger on the screen. Even though they found the baby and the heartbeat was strong, it was decided that I should have an amniocentesis. It was scheduled for week 17.

At week 14, I had a doctor's appointment. He told me that I wouldn't be able to hide it much longer. It looked like this was going to be a big baby. In a way, that was very comforting news. I never had to wear maternity clothes with Kelly. She had stopped growing at week 20. Getting big was good, right? I was trying to be positive here. I still wanted the reassurance.

I was not excited for the amnio. Maybe I was. We both needed some comfort and maybe a small guaranty that this baby would be healthy. There were some risks involved with an amniocentesis. Was it worth it? With our history, we agreed it was. The amnio was scheduled. The doctor who actually did these in Mason City flew his private plane from the Twin Cities. On the day the test was scheduled, there was a snow storm in Minnesota. We drove the 60 miles. Yes, we wanted to do this. However, the doctor was late. We waited close to 4 hours. The doctor ended up driving down from the cities. The weather was too bad to fly. As selfish as I was feeling, I thought he had BETTER be here. I didn't care about the weather. He had better there and get it done. Rescheduling would be a nightmare. As I said before, my work wasn't the best with the all the time I had to miss. But to me, this was my life. This was important. This wasn't a game or someone playing hooky. Thank goodness, the doctor did make the drive.

I went into the room to prepare. They started with an ultrasound. As the technician was doing the ultrasound, I pointed to the screen. There was a white line around the baby's head. I asked her what that was. She laughs and says it was the baby's skull. I said, not too nicely, I might add, "Good, because my last baby didn't have one." I wish I could say I regretted that, but I can't. Sometimes, people just need to be careful in their mannerisms and what they say. I was nervous. I was anxious. I was not in the mood for jokes. All I wanted was good news. They stuck the needle into my abdomen. I watched the ultrasound screen as the needle penetrated the amniotic sac around the baby. They pulled out the fluid. They then told me it would take 7-14 days for the results to come back. Those days would just fly by and be easy.

Yeah right.

During the wait, Bill and I discussed whether or not we wanted to find out the gender of the baby. At first, I said I didn't want to know. He said he did. He made the argument that it would be easier to get everything ready. We could have a room set up and clothes purchased ahead of time. I could see the practicality of it. I went with his decision.

On the 7th day, I still had heard nothing. On day 10, I gave the doctor's office a call. They said they didn't have the results yet. It was strange; they had everyone else's, but not mine. Are you serious? Then they told me it was nothing to worry about. Sometimes they just take longer. I was to just go about my day and try not to think about it. Well, that should be easy! On day 14, she called me at work! She told me that the tests were back and that the baby was perfect! She also asked if I wanted to know the gender. I almost said I didn't want to know, but I told her I did. She asked what we had at home and I told her we had a girl. She told me to go buy more pink! I was going to have a healthy baby girl! I hung up the phone and cried. I called Bill. I told him our baby was healthy. He asked if they gave the gender. I told him it was a girl. In my mind, he sounded a little disappointed. I guess every man wanted a son. After everything we had been through, could he possibly be disappointed? He really wasn't. I think he was just as relieved as I was. We decided, at this point, that we would keep the sex of the baby to ourselves. Only my mother knew we were having a girl. We made the comforter for her bed together. It was wonderful.

A couple weeks later, I was suffering from deep coughing issues. I talked to my Ob-Gyn doctor and they wanted me to see my family doctor. They didn't want it to turn into anything more serious. So, I went to the doctor. Now I will say the doctors in Algona were not my favorite. They always made it seem like going to them was an inconvenience. Not all the doctors, just a few. The one I saw was one of those that didn't appreciate the disruption. He examined me. He thought it was just bronchial spasms and prescribed an inhaler. I said that was good because I had just gotten the results of my amnio and it said the baby was perfect. What was his response to that? Just because it said the baby was perfect doesn't mean it would be. It could be missing an arm, be deaf or blind or any number of other physical defects. Are you frickin' kidding me?! I looked at him and told him that with everything we had been through, those were just details.

Nice bedside manners, Dr. Jerk!

Chapter 15

All this time, I was working at the insurance company full-time and part-time at the radio station. A full-time position opened up at the radio station. It was for a copywriter/producer. Could I do that? Oh heck yes! Anything was better than insurance. (Of course, that's just my personal opinion. Hats off to those of you who work with and love the insurance side of life. It's definitely not my cup of tea!) I interviewed for the position and I was hired full time. I would now be writing radio commercials, recording and producing them. I would record people who wanted to use their own voice. I would make out the part-time schedules. I would fill in on-air and do interview programs. Now this was a job that wouldn't put me into a coma by sheer boredom! The boss knew I was pregnant and hired me. It was two years to the day that I worked at the insurance company. My last day there was March 13, 1997. I was so excited to move on.

With this job came a lot of hours and every other Saturday morning. It was OK. I got to be creative. I was on the radio. Poor Bill couldn't even go to work to get away from me. There was only one radio station in Algona, so everyone listened to it. He got to hear my voice every day, all day. If I wasn't on the air, I was on a commercial. Things seem to be getting better. The pregnancy was advancing quite nicely. I was getting big and I was worried that the baby would be huge. After all my previous issues, I would take that!

I like names. I like to think about names. Since I used to be a teacher, I didn't like common or trendy names. I would have preferred for my children not to be one of three children with the same name. (Shayla was picked out when I was 16. I'm just glad Bill liked it!) We first started with Brianna. We liked it. The more I thought about it, the more I didn't like the way Brianna O'Brien sounded. (Now I'm really glad we didn't go with that. There are so many in her school.) I liked Olivia, but not Olivia O'Brien. We settled on Molly. That was until I saw all the graduation announcements in the paper and there were 16 girls named Molly. Scratch that one off the list. I had one that I really liked, but it was unusual. I threw it out there and Bill said OK. I wanted him to think about it, but he agreed. I was surprised. This one stuck. More on that later.

Everything was going great, right? Not so fast.

In July of that year, we were at my brother's house. It was his daughter's birthday, so they had a little family gathering for her. Shayla was out running around with the kids. (They lived on acreage. They had a lot of running around to do!) That night, we gave Shayla a bath and got her ready for bed. As we were putting her to bed, she had a seizure! It had been over a year since her last one! This had to be a joke! Off we went to the hospital. She was running a fever, of course, and had a slight ear infection. Damn. We filled yet another prescription. She seemed to recover quickly after this setback.

The next weekend, it was my parent's wedding anniversary. It was their 45th. They had a little get-together at their house. They had a really big garage and liked to have the gatherings outside and in the garage. It was a hot July day. They were serving food out in the patio and people were everywhere. We had family pictures taken. At the time of the party, I was only 3 weeks away from my due date of August 3rd. The heat was unbearable for me. I had to spend most of my time in the house and air conditioning. I apologized to my sister-in-law for not being able to handle it. I will never forget her words. "You're 36 and pregnant. What the hell were you thinking getting pregnant?" Words, people! Words hurt more than physical pain sometimes. You were at the funeral. You knew what we had gone through. I couldn't believe it. Count to ten before you speak. Will this hurt the person you are speaking to? If the answer is 'Yes', then open mouth and insert foot. Thank you very much.

After that hot July day, I had constant false contractions. I would scare people at work, especially our sports director. He was married but did not have any children. I would have to stop in mid-sentence and wait for the pain to stop. I think he was afraid I would have the baby right there! One time I was sitting in a chair talking to him and the baby rolled over. You could see it through my shirt. His face was absolutely priceless! The doctor said these contractions were due to the fact that I probably got a little dehydrated that day of the party. Since the baby should be big and we had an hour drive to the hospital, the doctor also told me that they would probably induce me at the end of July instead of letting me go all the way to my due date. I thought that was a good idea. I didn't want to have the baby in Algona or worse yet, on the way to Mason City!

It was soon August first. I had not had the baby and the talk of having me induced was over. Dang it!

So, my due date was August 3rd. Here it was, the big day. The day came and went and there was no baby. That night, however, I started feeling the pains. I was awake most of the night. The pains came and went. We decided to go to Mason City that morning. We called Mom and she took Shayla. The closer we got to Mason City, the pains got further and further apart. Since we were already there, we went into the hospital. I was put into a gown and told to walk the halls.

I was so frustrated.

After a few laps, I told Bill this was ridiculous. I would just get dressed and we would head home. He could still get in a half day of work. With this decision being made, we started walking towards our 'room'. The doctor met us in the hall. He said "There you are! Let's get this baby started, shall we?" Shall we?! Of course we shall! The Pitocin started around 10. That was awful stuff if you have no pain meds! I had nothing. The pain was very intense.

It really got things moving, that's for sure. It went too fast. The contractions were too close together. I couldn't have anything for pain. When I got to 9 centimeters, all progress stopped. The contractions didn't.

Have you seen "The Exorcist"?

I felt like Linda Blair. The contractions were coming so fast and furious, but I was stopped at 9 centimeters. The nurse told me to breathe through my next contraction. I honestly swear my head turned completely around and I spoke in a demonic voice, "YOU breathe through this one!" Of course I apologized to her. God bless the labor and delivery nurses. They had probably seen and heard it all. They are angels on earth!

They decided I wasn't progressing because my bladder was full. How would I like to make a quick trip to the bathroom? Sure, why not? Because it was impossible to move, that's why! We should try a bedpan. Yeah, that was not going to work either. Next step was a catheter. They inserted the catheter. My bladder was emptied. I progressed to 10 centimeters almost immediately. It was time to push!

Fifteen minutes later, at 4:34 p.m., Melaina Rae O'Brien was born! She weighed 7 pounds 15.4 ounces and was 20 ½ inches long. She was beautiful! The first thing Bill said, after giving me kisses, was, "This one has hair!" He was thrilled. I was thrilled. I was exhausted. It was different when I had the epidural. I had no pain. The stitching this time was different too. Phone calls would have to wait.

If I compared this experience with Shayla's delivery and post-delivery, this one was much better. You never knew what to expect the first time. I told the doctor about the excessive bleeding after Shayla. They came in to massage my abdomen a few times a day. I felt so much better the first day, honestly. I probably could have gone home that night. No meds during delivery made the recovery quicker. I stayed in the hospital. It was the time to get a little rest and sleep before we took the baby home.

This time, I was determined that I was going to breastfeed this child. All those negative comments about Shayla being sick because she was bottle fed still stung. I was not going to do that to Melaina. She would be healthy! The nurse brought her in to try nursing. She latched on! This was a great start! We "practiced" and supplemented with formula.

The next day, Mom brought Shayla over to see her baby sister. It was awesome. Shayla was excited. She got to hold her. I was feeling great. We would be able to go home tomorrow.

My grandmother, my mom's mom, told her that there was no way she was going to remember 'that baby's' name. I understood that it was not a common name. My mom, Elaine, told her that it was her name with an 'M' and the beginning and an 'a' at the end. I hadn't even thought of that myself. Having my mom's name in the middle of my daughter's made me love it even more!

We were able to take Melaina home and everything was going quite smoothly. Well, almost. At home, she wasn't latching on anymore. Again, there was no breastfeeding. We tried everything the books tell you. I went and bought a breast pump. That would surely get everything "flowing". It sure did not! Melaina was crying because she was hungry. I was crying because I was starving my baby. Bill put his foot down. He told me it was just too hard on everyone. Melaina would be bottle fed too. I tried people. I really did! No one tells you there is no textbook situation. Not everything goes smoothly when you have a baby. Unfortunately, some things were simply trial and error. I had always thought that breastfeeding was a choice. Either you did or you didn't. It was that simple. It wasn't.

Sometimes the choice was made for you. Mine was. It would be bottles for Melaina too.

At least Melaina slept! We would give her a bottle, lay her down and she would go to sleep. Yes, we got up every couple of hours to feed and change her. Again, God bless Bill. He loved to take his turn in the middle of the night.

About a week after she was born, Melaina started throwing up. I would feed her. I would wait about 10 minutes. She would throw up. Every time. Every day.

We took her to Iowa City. We were not about to go through a long medical journey again. They took x-rays. There were no physical abnormalities with her stomach. They diagnosed her with gastrointestinal reflux. We got two prescriptions. One was Propulsid. This medicine would help her digest her food quicker. The other was pediatric Pepcid. This would help her stomach pain. We took the medicine and gave it to her as prescribed. She really didn't like the Propulsid. It was a struggle to get her to take it. After a while, we took that out of the routine and continued with the Pepcid. She was doing much better. At least this did not require hospitalization or a surgery. A does of medicine when she ate was a much more manageable situation.

Right after Melaina was born, we got a card from our sitter. It said, and I'm paraphrasing, "Congratulations on your new baby. Find another sitter." As if we didn't have enough going on and things to worry about. I cried and cried. I was only taking a month off work because it was without pay. Two weeks after she was born we got this card. I was freaking out. Now what? We asked around and did find another sitter. Another problem avoided. I wanted to change my work hours to 10-6. That way I could stay home a little longer in the morning. Bill got off work at 4. It would be fewer hours at daycare. My boss agreed to it. After a month, I was back at work.

Besides the stomach issue that we now had a handle on, everything with Melaina was going so much better! She was happy. She was adorable. She didn't have a problem lying down. THIS was what babies were supposed to do! Ahhhhh....

Think again.

Chapter 16

At the beginning of January, Melaina started getting sick. I will admit that because of her sister, we were more than a little nervous when it came to her getting sick. I had to work on Saturday, so Bill took her in to see the doctor. He told Bill that she had a virus and there was nothing they could do. We took her home to see if we could ride this storm out. We put our couch and love seat together and made a make-shift bed, almost like a giant crib, and I slept with her on that for the weekend.

On Monday, she was not getting better. I stayed home from work and I took her to the doctor in Algona. He told me she just had the sniffles. I was told to let it go and I didn't need to take her in to see the doctor every time she sneezed. Thanks for making me feel like an idiot. I was not convinced, but since he made me feel about a half inch tall, I left. We slept in our little fort again.

Tuesday, she was not better. I took her to a doctor in Mason City. He told me that he didn't think it was anything serious, but he would prescribe her some antibiotics if I wanted them. Not really, Doc. I didn't want to pump antibiotics into my child if I didn't have to and if you didn't think they would work. We went back home.

Since I hadn't been to work all week, my mom said she would watch Melaina on Wednesday so I could go to work. Again, we slept in our little fort. I should say was the fourth night of sleeping in our little fort and I was not getting much sleep.

I went to work on Wednesday. I must have called Mom at least 10 times to check up on Melaina. My mom had 4 children. We all were sick at some point – including the old childhood diseases like measles, mumps and chicken pox. There it was again. That little voice that was screaming there was something more than the sniffles wrong with my child. I was a wreck all day at work. Mom called at 4. She asked what time Bill got off work. I said 4. Her response was "So he should be home soon?" I asked what was wrong. She said that when she went to change Melaina's diaper, she wouldn't wake up. She was breathing, but not responsive.

That was the last straw.

I asked if she could bring Melaina to my work and go and pick up Shayla. I also told her I wouldn't be coming home and asked if she could keep Shayla all night. In the meantime, I called the doctor's office in Mason City. I told them I was bringing Melaina over. I also asked if I should go directly to the hospital or to the office. They told me to come to the office because it was going to be during the regular office hours. We went in and saw the doctor. He told us that he was going to run some tests and see if she needed to be put in the hospital overnight. I told him that was not what was going to happen. He was going to put her in the hospital first and then run the tests. He had a rather shocked look on his face. He asked how long it had been going on. I asked him if he wanted to know the last time I slept because they went hand in hand.

He put her in the hospital "just for overnight". They gave her an i.v. and she didn't move. She was too sick. They did their tests. The nurse came into the room for a check on her about 1:30 a.m. She said, "This baby is going nowhere tomorrow. She is one sick little girl." I cried. Of course I do. You may think I'm a crier, but I'm really not. You will remember, I was raised with 3 older brothers. If you cried you were a "cry-baby". You were weak. I was not a crier - except when it came to my babies!

We found out in the morning that Melaina had R.S.V., double pneumonia, was dehydrated with a temperature of 104. Sniffles my ass! Mothers and fathers, please take this advice. I know I told you not to listen to everyone's opinions, but this is something very important that I learned over the years. You know your own child. Don't ignore your gut instinct. Don't let anyone else ignore you either! I was not happy. I was happy I forced the issue, but not happy that it was so serious! I tried to stop it before it got this bad.

I spent the next 4 days at the hospital with Melaina. Bill stayed at home with Shayla and went to work during the day. He would come over after work to see us. I didn't leave. I did leave once. Bill told me I needed a break and insisted I get out just for a little while. I think I was gone for about an hour. I was too scared to leave her. Melaina was highly contagious. The nurses and doctors came in the room completely covered from hair to the bottom of their shoes. I just sat in her room. They clipped oxygen to her bed. If she turned away from the oxygen, her saturation level went to less than 50%. It was a LONG four days.

She was finally well enough to leave. Shayla and I both got bronchitis. Mine was pretty bad, but I suppose that came with the territory. I would have taken it all if it would have spared her that misery of being sick!

We tried to get back to normal. I will say my boss was not happy about missing a week of work. What would you do? My infant child was in the hospital an hour away. I was not going to leave and try to work. I wouldn't have done a very good job and my mind would so be there, at the hospital. He never did get over that.

Too bad.

Even after that ordeal, Bill and I were considering having another child. Melaina had R.S.V., but she was getting better. If we wanted to have another, we couldn't wait too long. I was 36, after all. We thought about it. Maybe it would be a boy this time. There was an old wife's tale that says if you have 3 of one gender, the odds are about 75% that the fourth child would be the opposite gender. Yeah, I know. Tell that to the family that has 7 girls. It was a thought anyway. It was something to consider in the very near future.

It was now February. One day, Melaina started throwing up. Her temperature was 104. I called the doctor and took her back to Mason City. He did a check on her. He looked at her ears, nose and throat. He listened to her tummy and chest. He told me he couldn't find a reason for her high fever and vomiting. He did chest x-rays just to be sure.

We went back home.

The next day, Mom was watching Melaina again. Have I ever mentioned that my mother is a saint? I went to work. When I was out for lunch that day, the doctor called. When I got back from lunch, the receptionist gave me the message that I was to call and talk to the doctor. Not his office. Not his nurse. The doctor himself. I called. He asked how Melaina was doing. I said she was about the same. He told me that the x-rays showed she had a partially collapsed lung! She had so much 'junk' in her lungs that it was starting to block the passages. Are you kidding me?! He listened to her chest and it sounded good. We were to get her on antibiotics and watch her. It should clear up and no reason for another hospitalization. The babysitter didn't want her until she was better. More days off.

I remember, vividly, that one night I was changing her diaper. Bill was there. We had gone through more sleepless nights than I could count. She was my sleeper until the first time she got sick. It took Shayla 2 ½ years to sleep through the night. I was tired. We were tired. I looked at Bill. He looked at me. We both knew. There would be no more children. We were just so far past exhausted; we couldn't even remember what it looked like! I couldn't do the sick child dance anymore. We loved our children more than words could express, but we knew we couldn't go through this again.

Was THIS more than we can handle? Would this be our breaking point? Marriages had broken up with a lot less stress and hardships. It was no one's fault. It was just one thing after another. It was doctor's appointment and hospitals. It was sleepless nights. It was relentless. It was more money flying out for medical reasons than the money coming in. It was stunted fuses and exhaustion. We had short tempers with each other and little patience for much of anything else. Yes, we fought. It wasn't all sunshine and roses between us. Were we on the road to being a statistic?

Chapter 17

One night, Melaina woke up. It was my turn to get up with her. I took her downstairs. I thought I was all the way down the stairs. The last step was an 'air' step. I fell. I had Melaina in my arms. You don't throw the baby. I twisted and set her down. She was fine. She just sat there. I wasn't so lucky. I had broken my foot again and in a brand new place. Oh goody. That was 5 different places in 3 different falls. At least Melaina was unharmed.

I scheduled an appointment with a doctor in Fort Dodge, this time, to have my foot/ankle checked. I really wasn't too excited about the Spencer doctor. He made me seem like more of an inconvenience, even though the surgery was necessary. We scheduled another surgery. My cartilage was going fast. Arthritis was taking over my ankle. Already?! I'm NOT 50 yet! He was going to plate the break, clean the joint and drill holes in the bones. With doing that, they hoped to stimulate some cartilage production. Sounded like such a blast. Let's do this!

We did it. The surgery was scheduled for 7:30 in the morning. I was the first patient of the day. They got me in there a little early. That was better than waiting! The surgery lasted a couple of hours. I will say, though, I felt the best after this surgery. They gave me peanut butter toast and orange juice in recovery. We were on our way home shortly after noon. Ankle surgery #4 was in the books. There was a little crutch time, but the recovery wasn't super long. I was sure hoping this one was the answer to help with the pain and would let me be active for my children.

Speaking of surgeries, we had made the decision to not have any more children. It was time to take a permanent step towards this decision. I told Bill he was going in this time. I had had enough. He agreed. Or did he? He waited and waited and waited and didn't make an appointment. I didn't want to take birth control pills any more. I was tired of the waiting. I told him I would go in. I made an appointment to get my tubes cut and tied. After I thought about it, it wasn't a bad idea. I had had so many issues that I guess one more check inside wouldn't be the worst idea.

We went to Mason City for the surgery. We were to be there by 10 a.m. Again, we waited for 3 hours for the surgery. It was 9 in the evening before we got to leave. The doctor also told me that I had quite a bit of scar tissue. He would have cut that away, but he didn't have the proper instruments to do that. That wasn't the plan with the original surgery. It would have been nice to have it all done at once, but I guess things would be fine.

It was now time for déjà vu.

The ear infections started. Melaina began getting sick all the time. We took her to the ENT and they wanted to put tubes in her ears. It didn't really work that great for Shayla, but maybe it would for Melaina. We set up the surgery. She was such a little trooper. She had just turned 7 months old. She went in for the quick surgery. We had to wait around for an hour or so after so they could check her just to make sure she tolerated the surgery. We went to the cafeteria. You would never have known she even had surgery. She was bouncing, laughing, and smiling. This would be a great decision. She wouldn't be like her big sister.

She did have one incident. I went down into the basement to do laundry. Bill was in the kitchen and Melaina was on the other side of him in her walker. What I didn't realize was that I didn't close the door all the way. The next sound I heard made my heart stop. It was a crash followed by a scream. She had tried to follow me and fell down the 5 stairs into the mud porch. There was so much blood from her mouth. I called my mom. She came right over. We didn't know what to do. Since she used to work for a dentist, she gave him a call. We took her over right away. He did x-rays. The two bottom teeth that had just come in that week were gone. Completely. He told us there were three options: She swallowed them and we would get them back eventually, if you know what I mean: She inhaled them. That would be a horrible scenario: Or, they were on the ground somewhere. We called my dad to see if he could find them. He found them lying on the floor of the mud porch. We would have to wait and see what happened with these teeth. If the teeth would come in too early, the chances of them getting knocked out again were pretty high. They could come in twisted. That would mean braces. Or, her permanent teeth would come in when they are supposed to. (So happy it was the last option!) Other than that, things were going quite well. The tubes seemed to be working.

When will I ever learn?

I mentioned that I worked at a small town radio station. I had to fill in on the air. At 7 p.m., we would hit a button to go automated until 5 a.m. We had our last news report at 6 p.m. The person doing this report would be at the station alone. I was that person one night. I was reading the news live on the air and the phone kept ringing. I couldn't answer it. I kept hanging it up as I was reading. Finally, I came to a commercial break. The phone rang again. I answered it this time. If nothing else, it was going to tell the person I would call them back later. It was my mom. She asked if I had seen the ambulance go by on the highway. I told her I didn't and asked why. Melaina was in it. She had a seizure. NO! Not again!

But, that was the truth.

I tried to get someone to come in for me and close up. That didn't happen. As soon as 7 rolled around, I was out of there! I met them at the hospital. She had a fever with an ear infection. Here we go again. It was a horrible merry-go-round and the nightmare revisited.

She was released and home we went with our medication. I hoped that this would be the only one she had. How lucky are those parents who don't have to deal with this. Their kids didn't get sick and they slept through the night. We weren't so lucky.

After this, Melaina did not sleep well. She still wasn't sleeping though the night. From then on, she slept even less than before. She was awake with pain and ear infections. I remember taking her to the doctor. She had a fever and an ear infection. So, my favorite, Dr. Jerk, was the one she got to see. I told him about her seizure. He told me, in a very condescending tone, that he knew they are scary, but just let her have them. They wouldn't hurt her.

That night, she had another seizure. We went by ambulance to the hospital. Dr. Jerk was the one on call. He put her in 24 hours of "Acute Care". In this small town hospital, it was the same as intensive care. I thought they were no big deal. Why bother? Don't get me wrong, I'm glad they did. There was a nurse checking on her every hour throughout the night. I should know, because I never left. It just seems that there was a bit of contradiction there. Mark down seizure number two. Make this the last one.

Silly woman.

Melaina started walking at 10 months old. Her development was great. She was talking. She loved Barney and TeleTubbies. I don't even know why we let her watch them, but it kept her occupied and made her happy. Melaina turned one. For the most part, she was happy. She was a cute little chubby baby. She didn't like to wear her diapers and would just as soon go without. The funny thing is when we would put on a diaper; she would push it down to just below her butt-crack. She would walk around that way. We have pictures to prove that!

She wasn't always happy, though. It was the darn infections that we seemed to chase around. It felt as though we had been down this road before. We had. We tried to go on day to day like everything was fine.

A good friend that I used to teach with had a son that was getting married. We were invited to Rochelle for the wedding. I was excited to see these people and be a part of the day. We decided to take a long weekend and make the 7 hour trip. We would split the driving into two days. That would be a lot better with 2 small children in the vehicle. We had talked with our friends, Marc and Wanda. They had moved to Iowa City by this time and we would spend the night with them. It would be great to see them, spend some time and finish the trip in the morning.

That night, Melaina started running a fever. We tried to give her Tylenol, but she just threw it right up. The night was long and none of us slept very well. In the morning she was still running a fever. We decided to call Shayla's old doctor. The nurse told us that he was at a conference in Iowa City. It would be better if we went to the emergency room. We decided that was what we would do. We were checking in and the clerk was asking us the standard admission questions. We told her that she had a history of seizures. She typed that in. All of sudden, Bill shouted, "She's having one now!" She kept typing…she's having one now. If it weren't so upsetting, it would almost have been comical! Bill jumped up with Melaina in his arms and rushed her through the waiting room and back to a room. He didn't wait for the doctor to be available or have time to fit us in. This was his baby and she needed attention – NOW! A baby with a seizure got a lot of medical attention! We had 3 doctors, 5 nurses and a crash cart – STAT!

We waited at the hospital for hours. They wanted to see if she would have another seizure. They wanted to see if her temperature would go down as well. When they thought she was stable enough, they told us that it was just an ear infection and we could take her home. That's what we did. We took her home. We turned around, forgot about going to the wedding and just went home. We didn't want to be 7 hours from home in case it happened again. We had already had an ambulance ride in Rochelle with Shayla. Once was enough.

This was ridiculous. We needed another plan.

We took her to the E.N.T. that had taken Shayla's tonsils out. He said it worked for her sister; maybe it would work for her too. Let's take her tonsils out. Plus, while they were doing surgery, they were going to put new tubes in her ears. I was thinking that maybe, just maybe, this would be double assurance that all this crap of getting sick all the time would be over! She was just a little over a year and a half old! We didn't want this to keep going on. It did work for her sister. Maybe this was her answer as well.

We scheduled the surgery. Because she was the youngest patient of the day, she would go first. It was amazing how quick this surgery was! It seemed as though we had just sat down when they came in to say they were done. They were going to take her to recovery and we could go to her room shortly.

We got to her room and she was still out. The nurse told us that she started "fighting" it when she came out of anesthesia so they gave her a little something to knock her back out. This was about 9 a.m. It was about 11:30 a.m. when she woke up and threw up. She then went back to sleep. About 5 p.m., she was still out! Bill was NOT a patient man in the hospital. I was getting frustrated and he was way beyond that. They told us she couldn't go home until she was awake and ate something. But YOU knocked her out! Around 5:30, they finally let us go home.

At least her experience of having her tonsils out was better. After the LONG recovery room incident, the rest went fairly smoothly. She was always one to drink a lot. That was the key. She always had her cup, a popsicle or something along those lines. She recovered from her surgery quite quickly. That was a relief. FINALLY, no complications.

Was it the complete end-all miracle we were looking for? Not completely, but it was much better.

Chapter 18

About this time, I started looking for a way to make a little more income. My good college friends, Karla and Jacquie, were selling Premiere Designs Jewelry. I thought that maybe this was something I should do. I called Jacquie. We arranged to have my opening show and begin this business.

It turned out to be a great decision. I had a lot of shows booked and kept very busy. It gave us the extra income we were looking for, plus it was a lot of fun to go out and meet new people. It took my mind off the medical issues that we had been dealing with for so long.

Speaking of medical issues.

My foot was still hurting and swelling. It was painful to walk, sleep and even sit. We decided to go to Mayo Clinic for my foot. We had the appointment and Bill and I made the drive to Rochester, MN. They did x-rays and then we waited to see the doctor. He told me that I had no cartilage at all in the outside joint of my foot. But, he could fix it. All he had to do was saw off my foot, shift it and pin it back together! Are you CRAZY?! Saw my foot off?! I told him thanks, but no thanks. We took that information and went home.

The next day, I told my boss about what the doctor had said. He asked me what choice I had. If it would stop the pain, would it be worth it? Did he not know how scary that sounded? We thought about it again. After talking about it, Bill and I decided to go ahead with the surgery. We made the appointment. The doctor wanted to do it August 4th. I told him I couldn't do it that day. It was Melaina's 2nd birthday! He told us to have her party early. She was 2 and she would never know. He did have a point. We scheduled it for August 4th.

Bill and I went to Rochester the night before. We went out to dinner and I tried not to think of what was going to happen the next day. It was difficult. The doctor told me he was going to saw my foot off and reattach it. You try not to think about that happening the next day! It was not an easy chore. They told us to be at the hospital by 10 a.m. We were. As I have said before, Bill was not patient when it came to hospitals and doctors. It was a good thing there was so much construction going on. It kept him busy; watching that while we waited and waited and waited. I did not get taken to surgery until after 3! The surgery was over 3 hours long. They opened my ankle. They used a saw the doctor invented. They sawed my foot off my leg with this saw. It is shaped so they don't have to shave the bones to a curve, but it is cut that way. They shifted it slightly. They pinned it back together and put in a 10 inch rod that went through my heel, through my ankle joint and up into my leg to hold it all together. There were 4 plates, about 20 screws and more staples than I had ever had before, along with this rod.

I finally got back to my room about 9 that night. I woke up to morphine in my i.v. I told them I didn't do well with morphine before the surgery and to give me something else. Well, when I woke up to that, I was immediately sick. They told me I had to have something strong for the pain. They were right about that. I'm not a big one on pain meds. For this one, I needed it! Not only was there pain from the surgery, but I also started having muscle spasms. My foot wanted to be straight. I took pain pills and alternated them with muscle relaxers – one or the other every 2 hours.

After 2 days in the hospital, Bill brought the girls and they took me home. It was only a 2 ½ hour drive. But with the intense pain, it seemed a lot longer! I could do nothing for a long time. I was not even supposed to rest my foot on the ground. They did not want to risk pushing that rod into my leg. I stayed at home for a week. It was not easy having a 5 year old and a 2 year old AND being 100%

crutch dependent. If Melaina cried, I would have to find a place to sit and have her come to me. Bill had to do so much. He pretty much did it all. I know he got sick of it all. My mom came over and helped out as well. She would help with meals and laundry and check on me throughout the day. I tried to do as much as possible, but there wasn't much I could do.

I started going back to work after a week. I used my desk chair to wheel myself around. My foot hurt but I really should be at work. I ended up taking another week off. When I got back, we got into the routine. The receptionist opened the door for me and wheeled my chair to the door. I slid my way around the office and did what needed to be done.

I even kept doing my jewelry shows. I didn't want to take months off from the business. It would be like starting all over again. I had built the business and I had some great, loyal customers. I didn't want to lose that. My mom was not one for babysitting at night. Bill stayed home with the girls in the evenings and my mom went with me to all my shows. I was still crutch-dependent, so she carried my stuff in and set everything up. She was my "right-hand man" through all this. I did the shows and the talking, but she took care of so much. It was a great team effort. I thanked her with jewelry for as long as I remained a jeweler.

I had to go to the doctor three weeks after surgery to get the staples out and change casts. Mayo has a cast room. It is bed after bed of people with pins in their bodies somewhere. They took my cast off and took x-rays. As I waited, I looked at my foot. I almost cried or threw up or both. It was crooked. It was black, blue, purple, green, red. It was swollen. It was ugly! Then it was time to get the staples out. There were well over 100. Because they had been in three weeks, the skin had started to grow over them. I can take a lot of pain, but this hurt! I had to take a break and catch my breath half-way through it. The ones they took out on the side where I had lost feeling from my first surgery were the worst! The pain was really intensified there! They put a new cast on and told me to come back in a month.

I went back every month for a new cast. In December, they told me that they were going to take the rod out. I was dreading this. It was not a surgery. There was no pain medication. I could take Tylenol. They were removing this 10 inch rod in the cast room. I asked for whiskey and a bullet. They told me I couldn't have bullets in the hospital and thanks for the whiskey. Very funny. How was I going to handle this? I took a deep breath and I thought I was ready. They popped the washer off the bottom. Next, they took a pair of pliers and loosened the rod. The last step was have it just yanked it out! It was the most intense pain I have ever had! The only good thing about it was that it was quick. My foot "fell" to a position that I could walk on it, but not yet. There was more crutch time in store for me. Come back in a month for a cast change. In total, I was in a boot, cast, or crutches from August through April. Not fun!

I wish I could say that things were going smoothly for everyone after I was up and about from the last major ankle surgery. And, wouldn't that be simply lovely. It was just not the case. I really wanted to be free of medical issues. I had been without something on my foot since April. I was going to be healthy – especially for my children. I hoped my children were past the worst. They hadn't been sick for a while now, but with their history, you never lose the worry and fear from one day to the next.

Later that fall, I started having horrible pains in my lower right abdomen. Severe pains. Sorry to be descriptive here, but bowel movements were horrible. I would go about 6 times a day. I thought that maybe it was time to see my doctor in Mason City that did the tubal ligation. I made an appointment with him. He told me that the scar tissue had caused my bowel to be attached to my abdomen. I would have to have another surgery.

Oh goody.

First, however, I had to go in for a lower G.I. That was not pleasant. The stuff I had to drink was awful. That was out of the way and the surgery was scheduled. My doctor would be there and a general surgeon would also be on stand-by. My doctor would cut away the scar tissue and hopefully everything would just fall back into place. The general surgeon was there in case there had to be a complete bowel resection! My stay in the hospital could be non-existent to up to 2 weeks. Well now, didn't that make it easy to plan? The surgery was done and I got to go home later that day. No resection needed. Thank God!

I am telling you, those years were almost an endless stream of doctor's appointment and surgeries. If it wasn't one of the girls, it was me. It just seemed as though the madness that was our lives was overwhelming. So much of the pressure was on Bill. I couldn't walk for about 8 months. With a child and a toddler running around the house and me not being much help, he took care of the day to day – plus went to work.

Shayla was 5 by this time. She had started Kindergarten. Melaina was 2. She was at daycare. Things were going along quite nicely. Were the girls never sick again? No. But at least it was more manageable. There hadn't been seizures. There were the trips to the doctor. There were still infections. But, they didn't seem as overwhelming any more.

I had those last two surgeries on my abdomen and I thought that should take care of everything. You really would think I would have learned, wouldn't you? The cysts came back! It's crazy, but the ovarian cysts came back with a vengeance. One night as we were going to bed, I got the most intense pain. I tried to go to the bathroom.

That didn't work. I tried lying in bed. The pain was still horrible. Maybe the bed was too soft. I tried the floor. That didn't work. Maybe the carpet was too soft. I tried the bathroom floor. That didn't work. The pain was so horrible that the only option was the emergency room. We called my mother to come over to watch the girls. Once again, off we went to the hospital in Algona. They did a few tests.

I spent the night.

The next day the doctor came in and wanted to know who my OB doctor was. I told him my doctor was in Mason City. He told me to go to him then. Did this doctor really not want to help me because my doctor wasn't him? I thought they took an oath, but maybe these doctors didn't have to. Maybe they crossed their fingers. Maybe it was me. I didn't know what it was. They certainly didn't seem like they wanted to help. Did I want to be transferred by ambulance? I thought we'd save the $600 and go by car, thank you very much.

We walked into the doctor's office. The nurse took one look at me and took me to a room immediately. I couldn't stand upright. I was white as a sheet. The doctor told me that I had a ruptured cyst with internal bleeding. This was new. This was so not fun! I stayed there for a while. There really wasn't much they could do at this point. They just wanted to make sure I wasn't going to pass out and that my blood pressure didn't drop any more. Eventually, I was sent home.

Another month went by and there was another rupture and hospital visit. The next month brought another rupture and another trip to the hospital. After a visit to the doctor, I was told I had 4 options. Option 1: do nothing. I could keep having the ruptures and just live with it. No, thank you. Option 2: Have surgery about once a year or as the need arises. No, thank you. Option 3: be on the pill constantly. No, thank you. Option 4: have a hysterectomy. Even though I had my tubes tied, there is just something so final and frightening about a hysterectomy. I knew I wouldn't have more children, but the heart and mental state were a little conflicted. It's hard to explain. The thought of having kids was all-consuming for so long that it was hard to let go. Logic took over and a hysterectomy was the most practical choice.

First, though, I was told I had to take the pill. What? I really didn't like the side effects I was having taking them before having my tubes tied. I was nauseous and very irritable. Plus, I still had pain. The reason for taking them was to shut down my system so I didn't have a period. That was not the worst news I had ever heard. I took the pills for 3 months straight. I was ready. Let's do this already!

I had the hysterectomy. It went great. I spent one night in the hospital. For years I walked and stood a little hunched over. It helped to relieve some of the horrible pains I had in my lower abdomen. After the surgery, I had no pain. I couldn't believe it. I could stand up straight. I felt wonderful for the first time in a long time!

With a complete hysterectomy, you are supposed to take 4-6 weeks off. I called the doctor after a week and asked if I could go back to work. They told me it had to be a least a month. I told them that if they didn't let me go to work, I was going to start moving furniture! I felt that good! We agreed to half days for the next couple of weeks. As I was tired and still napping when I was at home, the doctor didn't think I was completely recovered from the surgery. The half days of work was a great compromise. I will say not having pain and being able to stand up straight was new and amazing!

It was great living close to my parents. In fact, during those past 5 years, I don't know what we would have done without them! Was it Divine intervention? I really felt as though God had His hand at putting us closer to my parents when we would need them the most. However, the small town living was beginning to close in around Bill and me. The lack of convenience was something we were really beginning to miss. I mean, we had to drive an hour in any direction just to get to a Walmart, and make a day of it, just to get things we needed. It was a once a month trip. If we realized at 9 at night we needed milk, it was a half hour drive round trip. We thought this was what we really wanted, but now we started to rethink small town living. And, there was the privacy aspect. That really didn't exist. Everyone knew your business. Even though I was born and raised in Whittemore, we still felt like the new kid in school – like an outsider that doesn't quite fit in.

I was still selling Premier Jewelry at the time. I had a pretty good business in Whittemore and the surrounding areas. I had wanted to expand my business, so I contacted a few friends in Cedar Rapids. They agreed to have some jewelry shows for me. That grew into doing more jewelry shows. We would have to travel to Cedar Rapids on weekends. The more we went back, the more we wanted to be back. Would it be a smart move? Would we hurt my parents? Would we find jobs again? We thought about it and talked about it a lot. I think the clincher for me was the time a neighbor asked me if one of the girls was sick. I said "Yes" and asked how they knew. They said because our lights were on at 2 a.m.! Why were you watching my house at 2 a.m.?

Shayla was in first grade by this time. Melaina was three.

Chapter 19

We decided to look for jobs back in the Cedar Rapids area. I sent generic resumes and cover letters to radio and TV stations in the area. I got a phone call almost right away from a radio station. We scheduled an interview for a Sunday. I was surprised they were willing to interview on a Sunday, but it really worked out the best for us. In retrospect, I think they already knew they wanted to hire me and the interview would be a formality. I went for the interview. I heard back pretty quickly and I was offered the job. We hashed out some details – salary and start time. We decided to put our house on the market. We had the realtor come over and told him that we wanted to do this very secretively until we could talk to my parents, but to get the listing ready.

The very next day, we were asked if we were moving. They saw Joe, the realtor, leaving our house. The secret was out.

My parents were not too happy about us leaving. It had NOTHING to do with them. They would have been the one reason to stay. The last thing we wanted to do was to hurt their feelings. We would have taken them with us! It was about our jobs, our future, opportunities for the kids, convenience! I went in to tell my boss, but he already knew. Why were we leaving again? We asked Shayla if she wanted to move. She wanted to do it immediately. She rode the bus home every day from school and was scared of the kids on the bus.

Bill also got a job as a driver for a concrete company. We went to Cedar Rapids to look for a place to live. We didn't want to buy right away. We still had a house in Whittemore to sell. Who knew how long that would take? (As a side note, it took about a year and we made $0 in order to sell.) We found a house we liked in Marion. A man came over to show it to us. We thought he was an overworked employee. We were so wrong! It turned out that we rented a house in Marion from the worst real estate company in town! Why wouldn't we? We always had the best luck! The house was ideal for us. It was on a quiet street on a hill. We had great neighbors. We moved the first week in May. It wasn't the best timing for school, but the jobs were starting and we had to go. (We had to move after a year because of the landlord's unethical practices. This landlord is now doing time in federal prison.)

Our friend, Vanessa, was doing daycare at the time. The girls would start going there. Everything was falling into place.

Shortly after moving, Melaina had her 4th birthday. Time was moving quickly! Next year she would be in kindergarten.

Meanwhile, my foot was horrible again. By October, I was really having trouble with all aspects of my daily routines. Sitting was painful. Sleeping was impossible. Walking was unbearable. I was a slave to my ankle pain. I went to see a doctor in Cedar Rapids. He told me my ankle was shot. Ankle replacements were not good. The joints were too small and there were so many components that had to adhere to the joint. Most of the time, the joint was too loose. That would make the pain even worse. That did not sound like something I was willing to take a chance on. My only option was to have my ankle fused. We scheduled the surgery. They had to saw my foot back off, straighten it out, file it down and pin it together. I would no longer be able to move my foot. It would now be permanently at a 90 degree angle. Didn't that sound like fun? My days of being active were completely gone. My girls would never know the athletic mom, just the 'handicapped' one. When I thought about that, it almost made me cry. I felt like I cheated them out of a fun and active childhood with me. I couldn't do all the things I used to. The pain was better, but it never went away completely. The recovery for that one was long as well. Unfortunately, I was getting used to pain and long recoveries.

After this surgery, I took a week off. When I went back to work, it was the same as before. I got into the door and into my office chair. Throughout the office, I would roll myself around to where I needed to be. It may not have been the most professional or graceful way to get through the day, but it worked. I didn't have to depend on others and I got my work done.

The next thing we knew, the summer was winding down and school was about to start. Before she started kindergarten, Melaina would have to have one of her tubes surgically removed. They usually fell out. But if they didn't, they had to be removed. We had that done. She was ready for school. I worried about her starting school. She would have been 5 for only a couple of weeks. Was she ready for school? Was she too young? Should she do AK (Alternative Kindergarten – for the young 5 year olds like her.)? We enrolled her in school. We thought that if she had a tough time in school, we could have her repeat kindergarten. But she was thriving. She was doing great!

I hadn't been feeling very good for a little while, but I really didn't think much of it. I had some stomach pains and felt a little nauseated. One day at work, I had to leave and run to the store to get some Pepto-Bismol. I took that and the pains seemed to ease a bit. Now as I look back on it, I think the relief was all in my head. I wanted to feel better, so I thought I did.

At my job, I had to do the billing for the radio station. This meant I had mandatory "volunteer" overtime. The paperwork had to be completed after hours. If the end of the month was in the middle of the week, the extra hours would be at night. If the end of the month was on a weekend, then I would work either Saturday or Sunday.

I was doing the billing one late Sunday morning. The pains in my stomach were horrible. I thought I should take a break and go home and have some lunch. Maybe I was just hungry. I ate lunch with my family and I went back to work. A few hours later, I really wasn't feeling well. I decided that whatever I didn't finish could be dealt with in the morning. I was starting to feel miserable.

I went home and had a few crackers. I made dinner for the family. I even baked some cookies for Melaina to take to school the next day. As that afternoon and evening wore on, I felt worse. It got so bad that I had a hard time standing up straight. It took Bill 4 hours to convince me to go to the emergency room. I relented. The girls went to the neighbors across the street.

We got to the ER around 9:00 p.m. and my blood pressure was really high - 185/130. That moved me up on the emergency list. They tried to give me an i.v. in my hand for the pain. The i.v. wouldn't go all the way into my vein. They kept coming in every few minutes to try and force it in. OW! I had a CAT scan done around 2 a.m. After that, the doctor came in and said I had appendicitis and walked out of the room. The nurse was there. I asked what that meant. Was I to go home and come back in the morning? She said, "Oh honey, you are having surgery as soon as the team is ready!"

At 3:30 a.m., I was wheeled into the operating room to have my appendix removed. At some point, I woke to the breathing tube down my throat and was choking! I don't know what part of the surgery…the beginning, the end or somewhere during the procedure…but I woke up when I shouldn't have! I was told that the appendix was leaking and just about ready to rupture! For three weeks I had these pains. I found Pepto-Bismol everywhere – in my desk drawer, my purse, my car, my nightstand and the living room end table. I'm glad Bill forced the issue of the ER.

I got home on a Wednesday. I went back to work on Thursday. I had no idea I wasn't supposed to. I went for a two-week check-up and the doctor gave me the approval to go back to work. Um, Doc, I've already been there! I also had a bruise all the way to my armpit from forcing the i.v. This was NOT a blue ribbon surgery for me. I did survive.

NOW everything would be smooth sailing! Well, not now...

There was a time when the other three, Bill, Shayla and Melaina, all had influenza. How it missed me, I'll never know! They were all home while I went to work. Shayla seemed to recovery pretty quickly.

One day, it was just Bill and Melaina at home. I was at work when my phone rang. It was Bill. He said he went to the basement to do laundry. When he came upstairs, he thought Melaina was just getting over a seizure! Are you kidding me? It had been years! This couldn't be happening again! He told me that he was going to call the doctor and then call me right back. I hung up in shock. I went to talk to my boss and told her what had happened. She asked why I was still there and to get home! I started driving home and my phone rang. It was Bill. She had just had another seizure. (That made five seizures in all.) The ambulance had been called.

I pulled up to the house and the ambulance was there. It was not a welcome sight! I climbed into the back of the ambulance with her. Off we went to the hospital. This was where I was grateful to be in this ambulance. I was so frightened of what my children had been through. I was amazed that Bill and I had made it through so many years of downs and not many ups. I knew she would get better. I didn't like it, but we prayed every time there was a seizure it wouldn't be life altering and brain damaging. That was when I thought about how we got here. Why were there so many trips to the hospital? I wouldn't want anyone else to go through that, but why did we have to? In the grand scheme of things, it was nothing that was fatal for the two girls. The medical issues were just persistent.

When we got to the hospital and she was checked out, the diagnosis was ear infection. Of course it was. She was seen by the doctor and we got to take her home later. Because of the 2 seizures in one day, they scheduled her for an EEG. Melaina was just the cutest little kindergartner and quite the social butterfly. She went back to school and told everyone she was going to have brain surgery! I also had to mention that her kindergarten teacher was fantastic. After this, she did research on what to do if Melaina had another seizure and it happened during school. Thank God she didn't have to use that information.

Melaina had her 'brain surgery' and it came back normal. Epilepsy was again ruled out. We were told she should outgrow these completely by the time she was 6. You had less than a year for that to be true.

They were right. No more seizures for either one of the girls. Shayla rarely got sick any more. In fact, it was almost 10 years after her tonsils were out before she got sick again. Melaina still gets hit with a virus almost every year. But that just runs its course.

After close to 15 years of struggles, hardships, tests of faith, and heartbreak, maybe now our Bradyesque journey can begin.

Chapter 20

Happy October 15th. So what does that even mean? For many, October 15th has no significance. For those that do know, it's not a day to celebrate. It's not a happy occasion. In 1988, President Ronald Regan proclaimed October as National Pregnancy and Infant Loss Awareness Month. If there is a child with no parents, they are called an orphan. If a husband or wife loses their spouse, we call them a widow or widower. What do you call a parent who loses a child? There is no word to describe them. This month recognizes the loss so many parents experience across the United States and around the world. The special day of Pregnancy and Infant Loss Remembrance is October 15th of every year. This inspired me to write. Not to gain sympathy, but to put down into words what has happened to me – to us. My intention is to give some, hope; and inspiration to others out there. You are not alone. You may feel like your world is upside down, not fair, and your dreams are out of reach. There are so many people out there with their own stories, struggles and heartaches. I just want you to know, that others have gone through it and survived. It is excruciatingly painful, but survival is possible.

When I look back on those years, I don't know how we did it. How did we virtually go nine years without a full night's sleep? How did we watch our children suffer and no one could help? How did we stay together? Infertility and the death of a child can certainly ruin a marriage. Plus, add in the medical issues I had along with the number of surgeries. Bill was always there. Bill was the rock. He was really the glue that held us together. We could have been a marriage statistic. Instead, our mantra was that we could do this. This will get better. WE will get through this. We don't have a housekeeper who can provide introductions to celebrities. We have each other, and that's enough.

It has been said, "God only gives you what you can handle?" I'm not going to lie. There were many, many days when I said, "I've had enough! I can't take one more thing!" To be honest, I don't know how we handled everything we were given. I've also learned to never ask 'what's next'. You may not like the answer to that question.

A friend, Ruth, from my radio days in Algona, told me I had a black cloud that just followed me around. While that may be true, I do believe the black cloud had a silver lining. There was always something not so pleasant happening, but we still managed to get through it. The lining was the strength of family.

When people have asked me how we survived all that we have gone through, I've always told them, "It's amazing what you can do when you don't have a choice." A little faith can take you a long way. Even if you struggle with it, don't give up. I don't think God ever gave up on us.

Somehow we managed to survive. Our marriage is still strong. It's not without its ups and downs. It's not without struggle. We work at it and manage to keep it together. Throughout all of this did we ever want to call it quits and end our marriage? There were times. The stress and tension just seemed too overwhelming. Our choice was to go through this together and remain a family unit. I'm forever grateful we both wanted it that way.

I ended up having 2 more ankle surgeries. (That's the count so far and 15 total surgeries.) I will always have issues with that. But I look at it this way; there are people with no legs. Who am I to complain? I can walk. I can't do as much as I used to do and want to do, but I still have 2 legs.

We have 2 beautiful and healthy daughters. We've seen them grow and thrive. We've been through break-ups and heartache. We've experienced bullying in high school and college (another full story on that topic) and survived. We have gone to soccer games and watched them play. Wrestling meets and football games to watch them cheer. We are their loudest and strongest cheerleaders. They are our world. We make it a point to go on some kind of vacation every year. We have driven from Iowa to Florida, from Iowa to Texas, from Iowa to California. We have flown to Hawaii. The time we spend together is so important to us. You may think a family of 4 in a van from Iowa to Colorado to Vegas to San Diego all in one week sounds like a horror story. It was fabulous! Making family memories really warms my heart. There was a time when I thought we'd never have it.

When the girls were growing up, we were approached about hosting foreign exchange students. We also took that leap. In total, we have hosted five girls. They have stayed with us from 2 weeks to 11 months. We had Tamami, from Japan, for 10 months. Risa, from Japan, was with us for 2 weeks. Maria came from Spain to live with us for one month in the summer. We had Svenja from Germany for 10 months and Rebecca from Germany for 11 months. It was a great experience and we love having these girls as a part of our family as well. (We did have a 6th student. She was from Denmark and we asked to have her removed from our home after 2 months.)

There is probably not a day goes by that I don't think about Kelly. How can you miss someone you never met? How can you love someone who never lived? I do. We all do. Maybe it's because of everything we went through that really makes me miss the possibility of what could have been. Every day I wish she was alive, happy and healthy. It wasn't meant to be.

Maybe this was.

Maybe this can help someone. If you are reading this, is it because you are experiencing something similar? Infertlity? Miscarriage? Stillborn child? Marital struggles?

As I have said before, it would have been easy for us to have been just another failed marriage. Marriage, in itself, is hard work. Add in everything else that went on and some would rather give up. The strength you can find in each other is your foundation and your rock. Lean on each other. Lean on God. Say an extra prayer or two. I know we did.

With everything else, the heartache of fertility and heartbreak of losing a child, don't feel guilty about what may be going through your head or your heart. No matter what you are feeling, it's OK. Your feelings and emotions are yours. Don't let anyone dictate how you should feel. Listen to your own voice. Work it out with your spouse. Most men are brought up that they aren't supposed to be emotional. They have to be the strong ones. Don't make them carry the burden alone. Be the support for each other. Talk to another support person if you need to. Please, don't let anyone tell you how you 'should' be or feel.

Happy October 15th. It's not a day to celebrate. I'm not even happy I know that day of recognition exists. If getting pregnant was easy and if we wouldn't have lost a child, it would just be any other fall day. This day has a special meaning. It's twofold for us. I wish I didn't know what it meant. But because I do, I hope this can help you. Maybe Mike Brady's words of wisdom would be, "Life is not easy. It is so worth it in the end."

Stay strong, my friends.

Acknowledgements

All the while I was growing up, I never thought that this would be my story. It's not something you can really plan for or even have even the slightest hint that this could be your reality.

While I wish it wasn't, it was.

All the while we were going through this, I had yearned for someone I could talk to or something I could read. I felt very alone. That is my purpose for this book. As if infertility wasn't difficult enough, the death of a child was overwhelming.

I had never heard of Trisomy 18 before it was thrust into our lives. Oddly enough, a girl I grew up with and babysat for as a child had a daughter with Trisomy 18 as well. Her story is different from ours. At one point when she was pregnant with her daughter, she asked if she could sit down and talk with us about it. It was a very difficult conversation. I had no answers. I just hoped that talking to us about it helped her in some way. It was then that the seed of writing a book was planted.

This has taken me years to write. The part about Kelly sat unwritten for a long time. It was too painful. With the thought of others, I started typing.

While this is a true story of our lives, some names have been changed.

It has been a long road and I have some people to thank in this journey.

I don't know if I would have been able to finish without the support and encouragement of my friend, Sheila Banning. She convinced me that this is a story that should be told. She reminded me of my purpose and that there is an audience for it. She gave me suggestions, but ultimately allowed the story to be my own. She has been my rock. She has been a saint with the patience of Job when it came to all my questions. She gave me the courage to see it through.

While still questioning myself, I gave the unfinished manuscript to my close friends, Jacquie Dierks and Karla Klingenberg. They each read the not quite completed version. They were both very supportive as well. Jacquie showed me that this story could also be very helpful to someone encountering marriage difficulties. I hadn't looked at it that way. That also gave me the confidence to finish. With their love and reassurance, I sought to complete my project.

This was a difficult journey to travel again. I love all of my family and friends that have been there for me – for our family. There is healing in these pages. I hope others can find comfort as well.

CPSIA information can be obtained
at www.ICGtesting.com
Printed in the USA
LVOW13s1727220718
584578LV00012B/529/P